GIORGIS RODRIGUEZ

GIORGIS RODRIGUEZ

De aedibus

Der italienische Architekt und Architekturtheoretiker Aldo Rossi verglich die Architektur mit den Wissenschaften. Wie diese schreite die Architektur voran, indem sie stetig auf bereits Erreichtes aufbaue und sich so weiterentwickele. Diesem wissenschaftlichen Aspekt dient diese Buchreihe. Seit 2000 dokumentiert sie die aktuelle Schweizer Architektur. Die Reihe wird in ihrer Kontinuität gleichsam zu einem Gedächtnis der Architektur, das die Werke dem Vergessen entzieht. Von den mit hohem Qualitätsanspruch ausgewählten Architekturschaffenden werden die wichtigsten Bauten festgehalten, ausführlich dargestellt und dokumentiert. Jeder Band dient auch der Reflexion über den architektonischen Willen, der hinter den Projekten steht. So sind in dieser Reihe mehr oder minder alle in der Schweiz wirkenden Architekturkritikerinnen und Architekturkritiker mit einzelnen oder mehreren Textbeiträgen vertreten.

Der Hauptteil in jedem Band widmet sich dagegen der Welt der Anschauung. So sind jeweils anhand von Bildern und Plänen einige bemerkenswerte Bauten dargestellt, die nicht einer routinierten «Produktion» entsprungen sind. Vielmehr steht hinter jedem Entwurf eine leidenschaftliche Auseinandersetzung mit der Aufgabe und deren Prämissen.

Heinz Wirz
Verleger

De aedibus

The Italian architect and architectural theoretician Aldo Rossi compared architecture to the sciences. Like them, architecture progresses by constantly building upon what has already been achieved and develops further in this way. Since 2000, this series of books has been dedicated to the same academic approach in documenting contemporary Swiss architecture. It therefore becomes a form of architectural memory, ensuring that the architecture is not forgotten. The most important buildings by each of the selected high-quality architects are presented, described in detail and documented. Each volume also serves to reflect upon the architectural motivation behind the projects. By now, more or less every architectural critic working in Switzerland has contributed one or more articles to the series.

However, the core of each book is dedicated to the world of observation. Images and plans present a number of remarkable buildings that are not the result of routine "production". Instead, each design stems from a passionate engagement with the task and its premises.

Heinz Wirz
Publisher

101 De aedibus

GIORGIS RODRIGUEZ

QUART

Didier Challand
DICHTE UND WEITE   6

HAUS IN DEN BERGEN, LEYSIN   16

KINDERHEIM UTTINS, YVERDON-LES-BAINS   20

ERWEITERUNG KOMPLEX MIT SCHULE UND RATHAUS, SATIGNY   26

STADTENTWICKLUNG QUARTIER VIEUSSEUX-VILLARS-FRANCHISES, GENF   38

KINDERHEIM SERVAN, LAUSANNE   44

APARTMENTGEBÄUDE, CONFIGNON   50

ÖFFENTLICHER RAUM AM BAHNHOF CORNAVIN, PLACE DE MONTBRILLANT, GENF   54

KANTONSSCHULE CHABLAIS, AIGLE   58

SCHULE BELVÉDÈRE, CHÊNE-BOUGERIES   64

HOCHSCHULE FÜR GESUNDHEIT, GENF   68

SCHULZENTRUM ES II, MEYRIN   72

WERKVERZEICHNIS   76

BIOGRAFIEN, MITARBEITENDE, VORTRÄGE, BIBLIOGRAFIE   78

AUTORENBIOGRAFIE, DANK   80

Didier Challand
COMPACTNESS AND AMPLITUDE — 7

MOUNTAIN HOUSE, LEYSIN — 16

UTTINS CHILDREN'S HOME, YVERDON-LES-BAINS — 20

SCHOOL AND TOWN HALL COMPLEX EXTENSION, SATIGNY — 26

VIEUSSEUX-VILLARS-FRANCHISES URBAN EVOLUTION, GENEVA — 38

SERVAN CHILDREN'S HOME, LAUSANNE — 44

RESIDENTIAL BUILDING, CONFIGNON — 50

PUBLIC SPACES AT CORNAVIN MAIN STATION, PLACE DE MONTBRILLANT, GENEVA — 54

CHABLAIS HIGH SCHOOL, AIGLE — 58

BELVÉDÈRE SCHOOL, CHÊNE-BOUGERIES — 64

SCHOOL OF HEALTH SCIENCES, GENEVA — 68

ESII SCHOOL GROUP, MEYRIN — 72

LIST OF WORKS — 77

BIOGRAPHIES, COLLABORATORS, CONFERENCES, BIBLIOGRAPHY — 79

AUTHOR'S BIOGRAPHY, ACKNOWLEDGEMENTS — 81

DICHTE UND WEITE

Didier Challand

Vom gesunden Menschenverstand zum Gefühl

Die Arbeiten von Timothée Giorgis und Juan Rodriguez weisen eine Dichte auf, die sich aus der Kombination von Räumen mit schlichter Geometrie und konzentrierten Proportionen in Grundriss und Schnitt ergibt. Vorplatz, Hof, Garten, Promenade oder Halle, Vestibül, Galerie, Loggia: Jeder dieser Aussen- oder Innenräume kann einen eigenen Charakter haben und gleichermassen bedeutsam sein, je nach Grad der Beziehung, die diese Räume innerhalb des Gesamtprojekts eingehen.

Paul Klee, *Steinbruch*, 1915
Paul Klee, *Steinbruch* **[Quarry], 1915**

Ein Hof ist ein Hof, eine Halle ist eine Halle, ein Zimmer ist ein Zimmer. Die Artikulation einfacher Formen mit klaren Begrenzungen erleichtert die Lesbarkeit des Entwurfs sowie den von den Architekten gewünschten Dialog mit der Bauherrschaft, den Spezialistinnen und Spezialisten sowie den Gewerken. Das Verwenden finiter und relativ autonomer Elemente ist für die Architekten ein multifunktionales Gestaltungsmittel. Dieser Ansatz ermöglicht es ihnen zum einen, für jeden Raum die Bedingungen eines Gleichgewichts zwischen minimalen Nutzungsdimensionen und harmonischen Proportionen auszuloten; andererseits gelingt es ihnen so, den Charakter je nach angestrebter Atmosphäre zu präzisieren.

Die daraus resultierende Vielfalt ist im Falle der Erweiterung des Gemeinde- und Schulkomplexes in Satigny offenkundig. Die Gesellschaftsräume, der Gemeinde- und der Ratssaal weisen allesamt die einladende Anmutung eines Versammlungsraumes auf, jeder jedoch mit einem individuellen Charakter durch die Modulation der Trias Form – Materie – Oberlicht. Beton, der sich wie ein von Helligkeit umgebenes Prisma an die Erde schmiegt, eine hieratisch kraftvolle Linienführung, die den Ratssaal krönt, oder warmes Licht, das in allen Schattierungen im kassettierten Deckengebälk aufscheint: Die Stimmung des erlebten Raumes verändert sich grundlegend je nach Status, Nutzung und Position vor Ort und im Grundriss.

Die Architekten oszillieren bei ihren Entscheidungen zwischen einem Bekenntnis zum gesunden Menschenverstand und der Suche nach der Art und Weise, wie Räume Empfindungen intensivieren.[1]

Regionale Lesart

Es zeichnet sich eine Verbindung ab zwischen dem Interesse der beiden Architekten für gewisse traditionelle Formen des Bauens, der Raumorganisation und der territorialen Einbettung einerseits und der Dichte als Paradigma für die sparsame Verwendung von Ressourcen andererseits.

Für einen Wettbewerb in Saint-Cergue, der auf eine Wiederbelebung des generationenübergreifenden Wohnens abzielte, interpretierten die Architekten den regionalen Typus des Landhauses neu. Indem sie die äusseren Enden seines traditionellen Mittelgangs durch eine doppelte Geschosshöhe betonten – eine «subtraktive» Geste, die sich erfolgreich und wirtschaftlich auf ein Umbauprojekt anwenden lässt –, schufen sie einen fliessenden Erschliessungsraum, der in der einheimischen Bautradition üblich ist und das Gefühl gemeinschaftlichen Lebens über zwei Etagen begünstigt.

Das Haus in den Bergen in Leysin tritt auf noch komplexere Art mit der regionalen Baukultur in einen Dialog, wobei ganz eigene Beziehungen zwischen territorialer Einbettung, morphologischer Einfachheit, typologischer Raffinesse und wirtschaftlicher Konstruktion hergestellt werden. Daraus resultiert eine vordergründig regionaltypische Physiognomie des Aussenbaus, dessen Sockel und Fassadenöffnungen sich jedoch teilweise von der traditionellen Formensprache lösen, um sich zum Hang und zur

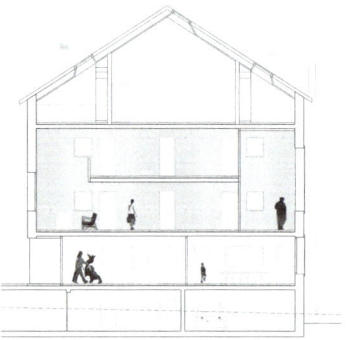

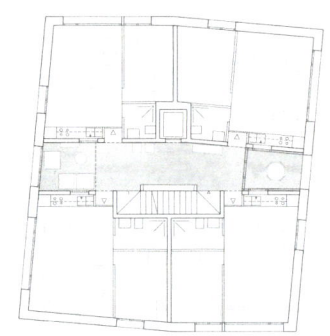

Kommunales Mehrgenerationenhaus, Saint-Cergue, Wettbewerb 2008, 1. Preis
Communal intergenerational house, Saint-Cergue, competition 2008, 1st Prize

COMPACTNESS AND AMPLITUDE

Didier Challand

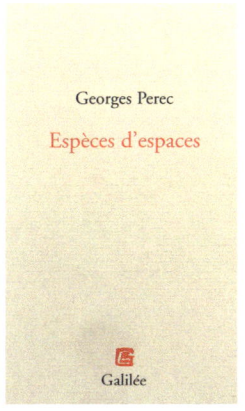

Cover des Buches *Espèces d'espaces* von Georges Perec, Paris 1974
Book cover, *Espèces d'espaces* by Georges Perec, Paris, 1974

From common sense to sensations

The work of Timothée Giorgis and Juan Rodriguez presents compact grains, resulting from the arrangement, in plan and section, of spaces with simple geometry and concentrated proportions. A forecourt, courtyard, garden, promenade or hall, vestibule, gallery, loggia: each of the exterior or interior spaces can take on a distinct character as well as equal importance, depending on the degree of collusion that links them within the coherent project.

A courtyard is a courtyard, a hall is a hall, a room is a room. The articulation of simple forms with clear boundaries enhances the legibility of the project and the dialogue desired by the architects with the project management, specialists and trades. For architects, the finite, relatively autonomous element approach is a multifunctional design tool. For each space, it allows them to explore the conditions of balance between minimal dimensions of use and harmonious proportions, and to specify the character based on the atmosphere desired.

The variety that results is obvious in the school and town hall complex in Satigny. The rooms for local societies and the community all have the welcoming quality of a meeting space, each with a distinct character, through the accentuation of the triad of form + material + zenithal light. Whether it is a prism infusing with light, the concrete that backs onto the earth, a hieratic line of force that crowns the council chamber, or shades of warm light in a coffered wooden structure, the tone of the lived space changes radically, depending on its status, use and position, both on site and in plan.

In this way, the choices of the architects swing between adherence to common sense and the search for how the spaces can enhance sensations.[1]

Vernacular lesson

A link emerges between the interest of both architects in certain traditional forms of construction, spatial organisation and territorial registration on the one hand and, on the other, compactness as a paradigm for the frugal use of resources.

In a competition in Saint-Cergue, aimed at updating the practice of intergenerational housing, the architects reinterpret the vernacular type of rural house. By marking the ends of its traditional central corridor with a double height, a "subtractive" gesture that could be applied happily and economically to a conversion project, they create a ductile distributive space that is familiar with the regional history and promotes the feeling of communal life on the scale of two floors.

In a more complex way, the Leysin mountain dwelling converses with the regional building culture to establish its own coherent links between territorial registration, morphological simplicity, typological refinement and economical construction. On the outside, the result is an initially vernacular appearance, but the base and the openings in the façade are partly freed from the ancestral language, sliding towards the slope and opening up to the sumptuous Alpine scenery. Inside, in a similar balancing act, the contemporary generosity of the spaces on the ground floor of the "mountain dwelling" contrasts with the "chalet-like" universe of the restricted sleeping areas upstairs. Pragmatically sophisticated, its wooden construction involves local, contemporary and ancestral expertise.

prächtigen Bergkulisse hin zu öffnen. Im Inneren kontrastieren die modernen grosszügigen Räume im Erdgeschoss des Hauses in einem ähnlichen Wechselspiel mit den im Obergeschoss konzentrierten Schlafzimmern mit «Almhüttencharakter». Für die pragmatisch durchdachte Holzkonstruktion wurde auf modernes wie auch traditionelles regionales Know-how zurückgegriffen. Die Kombination aus vorgefertigten Elementen und vor Ort realisierten Arbeiten erlaubte es, die Dicke der Wände zugunsten des Wohnraumes zu optimieren sowie die Innenräume und die Aussenfassaden im gleichen Farbton zu verkleiden.

Plastizität

Das Kinderheim Uttins in Yverdon-les-Bains bildet den Auftakt einer Reihe von morphologisch gegliederten Projekten, deren Plastizität die Erlebnisqualität des städtischen und häuslichen Raumes steigert. Hier erzeugt die Schlangenform des Gebäudes, die sich durch das Zusammenfügen von drei schlichten Baukörpern ergibt, Rücksprünge, wo rund um die mit Bäumen bepflanzten Höfe Intimität gefordert ist, und Vorsprünge hin zur heiteren Landschaft mit den umliegenden Gärten.

Kinderheim Uttins, Yverdon-les-Bains, 2010–2015 (Foto: Yves André)
Uttins children's home, Yverdon-les-Bains, 2010–2015 (photo: Yves André)

Der steinerne Baukörper des Kinderheims Servan in Lausanne führt den Charakter des Quartiers fort. Die Silhouette des an einer Strassenkreuzung gelegenen Gebäudes hat einerseits eine grosse Strahlkraft, gleichzeitig bietet sie aber auch dem Haupteingang und dem tiefer liegenden Garten Schutz. Die Dimensionen des gegliederten Baukörpers integrieren sich ebenso in das unmittelbare Umfeld wie die vertraute Physiognomie seiner Putzfassaden, die sich je nach der vom Grundriss geforderten Intimität öffnen oder zurücknehmen.

In Satigny dehnen sich die Prismen zwischen Dorf und Weinbergen aus, winden sich, ja werden sogar zerschnitten. Vor dem lang gezogenen Horizont holen sie tief Luft und blicken dabei auf eine weitläufige grüne Fläche, die sich geschickt in den Hang einfügt. Die Plastizität entfaltet eine konkave Wirkung bis in die Tiefe der Fassaden. Ihre auf drei Platzseiten variierende Physiognomie trägt zusammen mit dem abschüssigen Spielplatz und der hohen Platanenreihe, die bis zur vierten Etage reicht, zur Vieldeutigkeit des Ortes bei: Dieser ist sowohl eine Art grosses Wohnzimmer unter freiem Himmel als auch eine Agora ausserhalb der Mauern oder gar ein informeller Jahrmarkt.

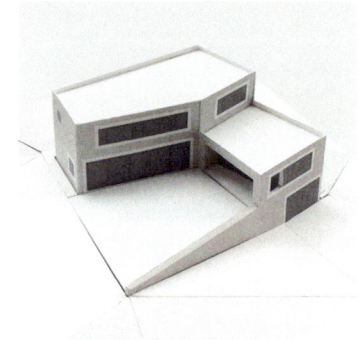

Privathaus, Grimisuat, 2012–2015 (Modell: Giorgis Rodriguez Architectes)
Private house, Grimisuat, 2012–2015 (model: Giorgis Rodriguez Architectes)

An wieder anderer Stelle erscheinen der Terrassengarten eines Hauses in L-Form (Grimisuat), die filigrane Erweiterung eines Gutshauses (Park Geisendorf) oder das frische Nadelkleid grosser Zedern (Confignon) als äussere Herzstücke des Projekts, welche dessen Lebensqualität im Inneren steigern.

Häuslichkeit

Häuslichkeit, von Timothée Giorgis und Juan Rodriguez als «Art und Weise, sich einen Raum gemäss der alltäglichen Nutzung anzueignen und zu bewohnen» definiert, steht im Mittelpunkt ihrer Aufmerksamkeit für die Wahrung des Ortes und der Landschaft, die kulturelle Dimension des Programms, die umhüllende Körperlichkeit ruhiger Formen, die haptische und chromatische Zuneigung zu den verwendeten Materialien.

Wohnraum des Experimental House in Muuratsalo, Alvar Aalto, 1952–1953 (Skizze: Timothée Giorgis, 1998)
Living room of the experimental house in Muuratsalo, Alvar Aalto, 1952–1953 (sketch: Timothée Giorgis, 1998)

Sie kristallisiert sich auch im Ökosystem des Grundrisses heraus. Die Einbindung des Programms als hierarchisches Zusammenspiel von Interaktionen in den kompakten Raumapparat fördert die Entstehung von intensiver besetzten Kernräumen, die mit ihren zugehörigen Räumen ein organisches Raumcluster bilden, das immer einen häuslichen Massstab aufweist. Ein System, das die Architekten von einem Etagenwohnhaus im Berliner Hansaviertel kennen und auch schätzen. Alvar Aalto hatte es für die Interbau (1955–1957) errichtet. Hier ist eine Konstellation von unterschiedlichen Räumen rund um den Wohnraum im Herzen des Grundrisses angeordnet.

The mixture of prefabrication and work carried out on site allows the thicknesses to be boosted for the benefit of the living space and the interior spaces and façades to be dressed in the same tone.

Plasticity

The Uttins children's home in Yverdon-les-Bains launches a series of morphologically articulated projects, whose plasticity enhances the lived quality of urban and domestic space. Here the snake-like form of the building, resulting from the addition of three simple bodies, generates folds, receding to create intimacy around the tree-lined courtyards, emerging towards the tranquil landscape of the surrounding gardens.

Apartmentgebäude, Confignon, 2019– (Skizze: Gabriela Pratas, Giorgis Rodriguez Architectes, 2022)
Residential building, Confignon, 2019– (sketch: Gabriela Pratas, Giorgis Rodriguez Architectes, 2022)

The mineral body of the Servan children's home in Lausanne continues the construction of the neighbourhood. At the street junction, it forms a silhouette that is both radiant and protective, for the main entrance and the garden below. The dimensions of the articulated body are incorporated into the neighbourhood, as is the familiar physiognomy of its plastered façades, which open or retract depending on the intimacy required by the programme.

In Satigny, between the village and the vineyards, the prisms stretch, skew and even shear. Beneath the stretched horizon, they breathe more, looking out onto a large green square neatly inserted into the slope. Plasticity operates in hollows, even in the thickness of the façades. Their changing appearance on three sides of the square, along with the sloping playground and the high line of plane trees on the fourth, contributes to the polysemy of the place, a large open-air salon, an *agora* outside the walls or a more informal fairground.

Elsewhere, the garden terrace of an L-shaped house (Grimisuat), the finely-structured extension of a mansion (Geisendorf Park) and the fresh foliage of large cedars (Confignon) appear as the external centrepieces of the project, refining the quality of life inside.

Domesticity

Domesticity, defined by Timothée Giorgis and Juan Rodriguez as "a way of appropriating and inhabiting a space, based on everyday use", is a key focus of their work to continue developing the location and the landscape, the cultural dimension of the programme, the seductive physicality of serene forms, as well as the tactile and chromatic charm of the materials used.

It is also crystallised in the ecosystem of the plan. The inclusion of the programme, as a hierarchical set of interactions, in the compact arrangement of rooms, promotes the emergence of more intensely invested core-spaces, constituting with their related spaces an organic cluster, always on a domestic scale. A device that architects know and appreciate from Alvar Aalto's Hansaviertel building for the Berlin Interbau (1955–1957) uses a constellation of different spaces revolving around the living room at the heart of the plan.

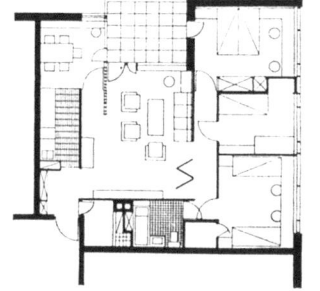

Gebäude im Hansaviertel für die Interbau, Berlin, Alvar Aalto, 1955–1957 (Foto: Heikki Havas, Alvar Aalto Museum)
Building in the Hansa Quarter, Berlin for the Interbau exhibition, Alvar Aalto, 1955–1957 (photo: Heikki Havas, Alvar Aalto Museum)

The spirit of this can be found in the residential building project in Confignon, where the open space of the living kitchens is the epicentre of a sequence linking the living room, the first-floor landing and the cedar garden. The standard layout of the Vieusseux-Villars-Franchises dwellings, at the competition stage, is also based on a cluster principle, with its group of spaces massed around a central entrance hall: four living rooms – six counting the loggias – drawing a constellation of relationships woven in diagonals.

The cluster extends, when the nature of the programme allows, to the third dimension. Landings fitted out, related transparencies, clear and soft light, a

Der Geist dieser Idee findet sich auch im Projekt eines Wohnhauses in Confignon wieder, wo der offene Raum der Wohnküche das Epizentrum einer Raumabfolge bildet, die Wohnzimmer, Etage und Zederngarten miteinander verbindet. Der Grundrisstypus der Wohnungen im Genfer Quartier Vieusseux-Villars-Franchises beruhte in der Wettbewerbsphase mit seiner Raumkonzentration rund um eine zentrale Eingangshalle ebenfalls auf einem Clusterprinzip: Vier Wohnräume – sechs, wenn man die Loggien miteinrechnet – erzeugen eine diagonal gewebte Konstellation von Beziehungen.

Das Cluster dehnt sich, sofern der Charakter des Programms es zulässt, in die dritte Dimension aus. Ausgebaute Treppenabsätze, zusammenhängende Transparenzen, klares und weiches Licht, eine Kaskade von Geräuschen und sich kreuzenden Blickachsen: Von der Treppe aus instrumentalisieren die Architekten die Durchlässigkeit als erlebten Verbindungsraum. Sie dosieren sie in einer Privatwohnung um der häuslichen Intimität willen einfühlsam, auf zurückhaltendere Weise und im grösseren, städtischeren Massstab in Schulen und Gymnasien.[2]

Palimpsest

Die Architekten orientieren sich an den bereits vorhandenen Spuren, an den greifbaren und veränderbaren der bewohnten Landschaft, an den immateriellen und erneuerten Spuren des Sinneseindrucks.

Das abseits einer Strasse gelegene Kinderheim Uttins interpretiert die bauliche Ordnung des Vororts auf kluge Art neu. Der Hof, den es zusammen mit den beiden Bestandsbauten bildet, stellt eine umfassende Schwelle zu dem geräumigen Haus dar. Das Leben darin erfordert Schutz und erstreckt sich deshalb zwischen den Bäumen in die Tiefe des Gartens.

Im Kontext des Genfer Stadtentwicklungsprojekts Cité Vieusseux erfährt der bestehende Kern des gemeinschaftlichen Lebens einen Zuwachs an Ausdehnung, Qualität und Bedeutung. Die sechs neuen Wohnblöcke, deren geknickte Gestalt selbst ein Erbe der alten Stadtform ist, stehen in Übereinstimmung mit den Bestandsbauten vereinzelt, zu zweit oder zu dritt, um im Zentrum einen würdigen Rahmen für gemeinschaftliches Leben entstehen zu lassen. Kontrapunktisch hierzu stellen vier ausgedehnte taschenartige, baumbestandene Ausbuchtungen die Verbindung zum urbanen Umfeld her.

Die domestizierte Topografie des Weinbergs bildet die Grundlage für die Gestaltung des Projekts in Satigny. Der lang gestreckte flache Baukörper aus lehmfarbenem Beton, der sich an das Terrain schmiegt und die Gemeinschaftsräume beherbergt, säumt den Hang und bewahrt den Ausblick. Die vertikalen Holzfensterrahmen erinnern an die Weinstöcke, die über der dicken Deckplatte aufgereiht sind, welche zugleich als Dach, als Ziergarten und als «möblierte» Promenade dient. Der am Rande der Grünflächen gelegene Gemeindesaal mutet wie ein lauerndes Tier an, wie ein unwahrscheinlicher Findling oder ein landwirtschaftlicher Schuppen, der mit einem eleganten Moirégewebe verkleidet ist.

Der landschaftliche Kontext lässt die Innenräume des Hauses in den Bergen in Leysin tiefer atmen. Durch die Öffnung der Fassaden im Wohnraum wird der rechteckige Grundriss in zwei Unterräume unterteilt, in denen jeweils ein grosses Fenster die Aussicht auf die überwältigende Landschaft freigibt. Umgekehrt sorgt die Sitzbank an der holzverkleideten Innenwand dafür, dass Körper und Sinne sich zum schwarzen gusseisernen Ofen hin ausrichten: Auf die romantischen Empfindungen der gewaltigen Natur folgen die archaischen Wonnen der Feuerstelle.

Baumstruktur

Ausgehend vom Cluster als organischer Struktur, die der Häuslichkeit förderlich ist, veranschaulichen die Projekte des Schulkomplexes in Meyrin und der Kantonsschule

Stadtentwicklung des Quartiers Vieusseux-Villars-Franchises, Genf, Abschnitt 1, 2017–2021 (Foto: Roger Frei)
Urban development, Vieusseux-Villars-Franchises neighbourhood, Geneva, Section 1, 2017–2021 (photo: Roger Frei)

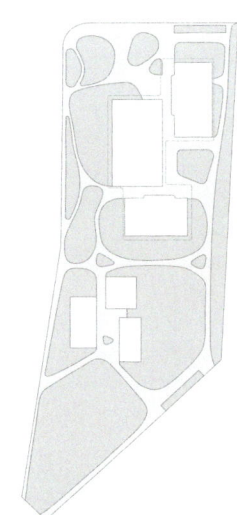

Schulzentrum ES II, Meyrin, Wettbewerb 2019, 3. Preis
Grundrissschema des Projekts unter Wahrung der bestehenden natürlichen Landschaft
**ESII school centre, Meyrin, competition 2019, 3rd Prize
Floor plan diagram of the project, respecting the existing natural landscape**

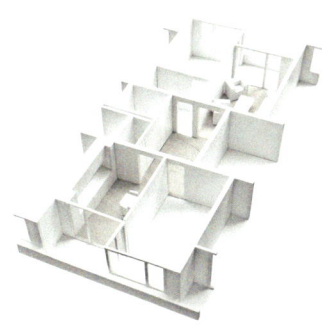

Stadtentwicklung des Quartiers Vieusseux-Villars-Franchises, Genf, Wettbewerb 2013, 1. Preis
Studienmodell der Typologie mit zentralem Eingangsbereich
**Urban development, Vieusseux-Villars-Franchises neighbourhood, Geneva, competition 2013, 1ˢᵗ Prize
Typology study model with central entrance hall**

Erweiterung Komplex mit Schule und Rathaus, Satigny, Abschnitt 1 (Gemeinde- und Gesellschaftsräume), 2016–2018 (Foto: Laura Keller)
School and Town Hall complex extension, Satigny, Section 1 (community and common rooms), 2016–2018 (photo: Laura Keller)

cascade of sounds and crossed views: from the stairs, the architects use the permeability as an instrument, as an experienced connecting space. They qualify this with sensitivity, in a more reserved mode in a private apartment for the sake of domestic intimacy, and on a larger, urban scale in primary and secondary schools.[2]

Palimpsest

The architects use pre-existing patterns, the tangible and alterable traces of the inhabited landscape, as well as immaterial and renewed sensory experiences.

Set back from an avenue, the Uttins children's home subtly reinterprets the built order of the suburb. The courtyard it forms with two existing houses offers a generous threshold to the "big house", whose domestic life, requiring protection, stretches between the trees in the depth of the garden.

In the context of the Cité Vieusseux urban development project in Geneva, the pre-existing core of community life gains in extent, quality and importance. The six new housing blocks, whose folded shape is itself inherited from the old urban form, are arranged singly, in twos or threes based on the existing buildings to create a large "framework" for communal living in the centre, juxtaposed to which four large pockets weave tree-linked links with the urban neighbourhoods.

The domesticated topography of the vineyard slope underpins the shape of the Satigny project. Set against the earth, in clay-coloured concrete, the long, low body of the social rooms skirts the slope while preserving the view. Its woodwork is reminiscent of the vines aligned above the thick slab, which serves as a roof, a pleasure garden and a "furnished" promenade. At the edge of the meadows, the community hall evokes an animal cowering, an unlikely drift boulder or a farm shed elegantly clad in moiré fabric.

The landscape context intensifies the inner breath of the mountain house in Leysin. The control of façade openings in the living room subdivides the stretched rectangular plan into two sub-spaces, each with a large glass panel overlooking the sublime distance. At a reverse angle, the bench against the wooded wall of the façade directs the body and the senses towards the black cast iron stove: the romantic feeling of the immense nature is echoed by the archaic delights of the home.

Arborescence

The Meyrin school complex and Chablais High School projects illustrate the porous, malleable, interactive, flexible and additive nature of the cluster as an organic structure conducive to domesticity, and the art with which architects use it to give meaning, orientation and hierarchy to complex buildings.

On the scarred relief of a partly filled-in quarry, the project in Meyrin addresses the theme of the ambivalence of a place on the boundary between the residential fabric of the satellite town and its surroundings, which are still agricultural, under a sky vibrating with low-flying aircraft due to the nearby airport. The architects maintain the rural character of the site by preserving part of the existing embankments and forest in the new network of courtyards and squares. Conversely, the straight walkways linking the main entrances, which can be seen through the sports-hall windows, are reminiscent of a pleasant covered walkway in an urban environment. As if by iteration, the complex universe of the project seems to emanate from the existing landscape and fertilise it in return, as illustrated by the tree-like cross-section, with its earth-infusing programme, its three prismatic bodies on the ground floor and the curved foliage of the patio floors.

Chablais in Aigle ausserdem die durchlässige, anpassungsfähige, interaktive, nachgiebige, additive Natur; sowie die Kunst, mit der die Architekten sie sich zunutze machen, um komplexen Gebäuden Bedeutung, Orientierung und eine hierarschische Struktur zu verleihen.

Auf dem unebenen Gelände einer teilweise aufgefüllten Kiesgrube thematisiert der Entwurf für Meyrin die Ambivalenz eines Ortes, an dem das Wohngefüge der Satellitenstadt auf eine noch ländlich geprägte Umgebung trifft und der Himmel von den aufgrund der Flughafennähe tief fliegenden Flugzeugen vibriert. Indem die Architekten einen Teil der Böschungen und des existierenden Waldes in diesem Netz von neu konzipierten Höfen und kleinen Plätzen erhalten, bewahren sie den ländlichen Charakter des Ortes. Umgekehrt erinnert die gerade Wegführung, welche die Haupteingänge miteinander verbindet und von der Turnhalle eingesehen werden kann, an die Annehmlichkeit einer überdachten Passage, wie man sie sonst im städtischen Umfeld findet. Das komplexe Universum des Entwurfs scheint wie durch Iteration aus dem bestehenden Landschaftsgerüst hervorzugehen und es im Gegenzug zu befruchten, was der baumartige Zuschnitt veranschaulicht: Aus der Erde heraus entwickeln sich seine drei prismatischen Baukörper im Erdgeschoss und die Blattkrone erstreckt sich auf die Geschosse mit den Patios.

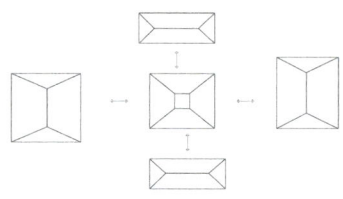
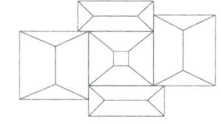

Erweiterung Komplex mit Schule und Rathaus, Satigny, Abschnitt 3 (Schulzentrum), 2022– (laufend) Schulzentrum: Konzeptschema der Kombination zweier Typen von Baukörpern, die in den benachbarten Dörfern häufig anzufinden sind
School and Town Hall complex extension, Satigny, Section 3 (school centre), 2022– (ongoing). School centre: conceptual scheme combining two types of structures that recur in the neighbouring villages

Die Kantonsschule Chablais ist als asymmetrische Gruppe von vier Baukörpern konzipiert, wodurch das Gebäude, gemäss den Architekten, zwar weniger lang ist, dafür aber stärker in die Breite ausstrahlt und leichter wirkt. Der gegliederte Bau verbirgt in dieser aus Hallen, Villen und Bahngleisen bunt zusammengewürfelten Landschaft seine Organisation rund um eine grosse Halle im Erdgeschoss und um drei baumbestandenen Innenhöfe in den Obergeschossen. Diese grossen, zentrierten Aussparungen setzen sich in der Baumstruktur fort: Die breiten, senkrechten Gängen sind zum Park und zu den in der Ferne liegenden Bergen hin ausgerichtet. Natürliches Licht fällt durch grosse Glaswände und geschickt dosierte Oberlichter ins Innere und färbt dieses entsprechend ein. Ausserdem rhythmisiert es die Raumabfolgen, die sich abwechselnd nach innen und nach aussen wenden, sich zurückziehen und ausdehnen, Gartenhöfe und belebte Hallen sind. Die Szenografie erinnert an «das Haus als Weg und Platz»,[3] an den schmalen Weg eines englischen Gartens, an den mäanderförmigen Verlauf eines Flusses oder, um mit den Worten der Architekten zu sprechen, an ein «Organ, dessen Atmung den Rhythmus des Lebens im Park bestimmt».

Montessori-Schule (Apollo-Schulen), Amsterdam, Hermann Hertzberger, 1980–1983 (Quelle: www.ahh.nl; Fotos: Ger van der Vlugt, Johan van der Keuken, Ronald Roozen und Klaus Kinold)
Montessori School (Apollo Schools), Amsterdam, Hermann Hertzberger, 1980–1983 (source: www.ahh.nl; photos: Ger van der Vlugt, Johan van der Keuken, Ronald Roozen and Klaus Kinold)

Zwischenorte

In der Dichte des Plans, der Wand, der Fassade wandeln die Architekten die Position, die Proportionen und das Material der Elemente ab – Überdachungen, Schwellen, Pfosten oder andere Stürze –, um den begrenzten und entscheidenden Raum zwischen zwei Orten zu verbinden, die mitunter zwei Welten darstellen.

Behutsam variieren sie Form und Charakter der Öffnungen, wenn nötig auch in ein und demselben Zimmer, etwa in Leysin, wo zwei grosszügige Fenster die Landschaft einrahmen – das eine eine feine, leuchtende Leinwand, das andere ein behaglicher, häuslicher Raum.

In Satigny erweitert eine tiefe, breite Schwelle, eingefasst in massive Eiche, elegant den Eingang des neuen Gemeindesaals. In diesem stehen sich zwei grosse Panoramafenster einander gegenüber. Sie geben sich diskret und lenken den Blick zum Horizont und in die Landschaft. An der Decke fächert sich die Holzstruktur in wabenförmige Zellen auf, durch die sanft das Licht einfällt.

Kinderheim Servan, Lausanne, 2017–2019 (Foto: Roger Frei)
Servan children's home, Lausanne, 2017–2019 (photo: Roger Frei)

Die Sorgfalt, die der Gestaltung von mitunter sogar vernachlässigbar erscheinenden Eingangsräumen zukommt, zeugt von der Leidenschaft der Architekten für die richtigen Verbindungen und Beziehungen auf allen Ebenen des Projekts.

The Chablais High School is designed as an asymmetrical agglomeration of four volumes, with the effect of "making the building less long, more radiant and lighter". On the heterogeneous plain, with halls, villas and railways, this articulated volume conceals the fact that it gravitates around a large hall on the ground floor and around three tree-lined courtyards on the upper floors. These major, centred recesses are extended by arborescence into wide perpendicular corridors, leaning towards the park and the mountains in the distance. Natural light colours the interior landscape through the large glass walls and finely measured zenithal openings. It also beats out the rhythm of the spatial sequences, alternating introversion and extroversion, constrictions and expansions, garden patios and inhabited halls. The scenography reminds one of "the house as a path and a place",[3] the loosened path of an English garden, the meander of a river or, in the words of the architects, an "organ whose breaths give rhythm to the life of the park".

In-between

Within the thickness of the plan, the wall, the façade, the architects combine the position, proportions and material of the elements porches, thresholds, jambs or other lintels to precisely shape the narrow and significant space linking two places, which are sometimes two different worlds.

Carefully, they vary the shape and character of the openings, in the same room, if necessary, as in Leysin, where two generous windows frame the landscape, one a fine luminous canvas, the other a comfortable domestic space.

In Satigny, a deep, wide sill, framed in solid oak, nobly enlarges the entrance to the new community hall. In this hall, the two panoramic windows stretch out opposite each other. They have a low profile, directing one's gaze towards the horizon and the land. On the ceiling, the queen membrane of the wooden framework spreads out its cells, from which the soft light glows.

The care taken in the design of the opening spaces, sometimes so tenuous as to seem negligible, demonstrates the architects' passion for the right assemblies and relationships, at all scales of the project.

The modulation of the link between inner and outer spaces is even more important in projects where, as in the Servan children's home there is an increased need for intimacy and a desire, if not for radiance, at least for openness to the setting of the neighbourhood. Three devices converge to substantiate the desired balance: the expansive nature of the three-winged building, the generous size of the bay windows in the areas less exposed to the street, and ultimately the regular mesh of the window frames. These light-coloured frames, which allow the mineral mass to breathe by unifying the different dimensions of the openings, have a distinctive bevelled side face to the right of the rooms, thereby enhancing the intimacy of the room by narrowing its opening and opening up the doorway towards the town.

Osmosis

"We design the project in its most concentrated form, to then explore the modalities of its generosity."

A space compact in itself, constricted and concentrated, can fuse into scale with other spaces thanks to the membrane, more or less ample and transparent, of a door, a bay or a window. Osmosis at work, on the domestic scale of the cluster or on the more urban or landscape scale of a wider context, has the effect of expanding the factual limits of the built space.

Kantonsschule Chablais, Aigle, Wettbewerb 2021, 1. Preis
«Verzweigtes» Konzeptschema
**Chablais High School, Aigle, competition 2021, 1st Prize
"Branched" concept diagram**

Kinderheim Servan, Lausanne, 2017–2019 (Foto: Roger Frei)
Servan children's home, Lausanne, 2017–2019 (photo: Roger Frei)

Die Modulation der Verbindung zwischen Innen- und Aussenräumen ist noch ausgeprägter bei jenen Projekten, bei denen – wie im Fall des Kinderheims Servan – ein gesteigertes Bedürfnis nach Privatsphäre und der Wille, wenn nicht nach Ausstrahlung, so doch wenigstens nach Öffnung zum Quartier aufeinandertreffen. Drei Elemente wirken zusammen, um das erstrebte Gleichgewicht zu erreichen: die Weitläufigkeit des dreigliedrigen Gebäudes, die sehr grossen Glasfenster an Stellen, die von der Strasse nicht so stark einzusehen sind, und schliesslich das regelmässige Netz von Fensterrahmungen. Diese hellen Rahmen, die die Gesteinsmasse atmen lassen, indem sie unterschiedlich grosse Öffnungen zu einer Einheit verbinden, stellen eine Besonderheit für die dahinterliegenden Räume dar: Sie weisen eine abgeschrägte Seitenfläche auf, die einerseits die Fensteröffnung des betreffenden Zimmers verengt und somit dessen Intimität erhöht, andererseits aber die optische Öffnung zur Stadt hin erweitert.

Stadtentwicklung des Quartiers Vieusseux-Villars-Franchises, Genf, Abschnitt 1, 2017–2021 (Foto: Roger Frei)
Urban development, Vieusseux-Villars-Franchises neighbourhood, Geneva, Section 1, 2017–2021 (photo: Roger Frei)

Osmose

«Wir gestalten den Entwurf in Richtung seiner konzentriertesten Form, um dann die Modalitäten seiner Grosszügigkeit zu erforschen.» – Ein kompakter, in sich geschlossener, konzentrierter Raum kann durch die mehr oder weniger grosse und transparente Membran einer Tür, eines Erkers oder eines Fensters mit anderen Räumen in Verbindung treten. Die Osmose, die auf der häuslichen Ebene des Clusters oder auf der städtischen oder landschaftlichen Ebene eines grösseren Kontextes stattfindet, erweitert die faktischen Grenzen des gebauten Raumes.

Durch einen solchen Austausch befinden sich die Räume im Gleichgewicht, werden zur Geltung gebracht oder verleihen sich gegenseitig Farbe. Sie bilden ein organisches Gefüge, dessen Charakter je nach Intensität und Vielseitigkeit der Nutzung, der Tageszeit und Stimmung der Orte, aus denen sich die Cluster zusammensetzen, und mitunter sogar je nach der sich verändernden Geografie des Clusters selbst schwankt. In der Wohnung, welche die Nordwestecke des ersten in Vieusseux errichteten Gebäudes einnimmt, stellt der Wohnraum a priori das bewohnte Epizentrum dar, ist jedoch durch räumliche und geometrische Resonanz gleichzeitig der Satellit des grossen Hofs, der selbst wiederum das Epizentrum eines anderen Clusters ist, in diesem Fall auf städtischer Ebene.

Ein Hof ist ein Hof, eine Halle ist eine Halle, ein Zimmer ist ein Zimmer. Die ersonnenen und erfahrenen Architekturen von Timothée Giorgis und Juan Rodriguez kultivieren eine «einvernehmliche» Zuneigung zum gelassenen Dialog zwischen den Menschen, Gesten und Dingen des täglichen Lebens und sehen darin einen Akt der Kultur, eine urbane Manier. Doch wie das Wort «einvernehmlich» selbst sind diese Architekturen gleichzeitig Trägerinnen einer weniger direkt geteilten Bedeutung.[4] Sie verkörpern eine intensive und andächtige Suche nach dem, was Sinn und Gefühl ausmacht, nach dem, was uns als Akt der Kultur anspricht und uns *zugleich* als Körper bewegt.

1   Bezüglich der Inspirationen für ihre Recherchen nennen sie einen Text von Martin Steinmann: «Sinnliche Dichte – Die neue Bedeutung eines alten Haustyps», in: *Werk, Bauen + Wohnen*, Nr. 10, 2002, S. 64–69.
2   Betreffend der vertikalen Erschliessung als Herzstück der Nutzung beziehen sich Timothée Giorgis und Juan Rodriguez gern auf die Schulprojekte Herman Hertzbergers, insbesondere auf die Apollo-Schulen in Amsterdam (1980–1983).
3   Josef Frank, «Das Haus als Weg und Platz», in: *Der Baumeister*, Nr. 8, 1931, S. 316–323.
4   «Einvernehmlicher Reflex: Reflex, der gleichzeitig in den beteiligten Organen entsteht, wenn nur eines davon stimuliert wird», https://www.cnrtl.fr/definition/consensuel (Übersetzung; letzter Zugriff: 8. Februar 2023)

Such exchanges result in spaces that balance, enhance or colour each other. They form an organic fabric whose character fluctuates depending on the intensity and variety of potential uses, the time of day and the mood of the places making up the clusters concerned, and sometimes even depending on the shifting geography of the cluster itself. In the apartment occupying the north-east corner of the first building constructed at Vieusseux, the living room is basically the inhabited epicentre. Yet by spatial and geometric resonance, it is simultaneously the satellite of the large courtyard, itself the epicentre of another cluster that has an urban scale.

A courtyard is a courtyard, a hall is a hall, a room is a room. Timothée Giorgis and Juan Rodriguez's conceived and lived architectures cultivate a "consensual" affection for the serene dialogue between the people, gestures and things of everyday life, seeing this as an act of culture, an urban way. But like the word "consensual" itself, these architectures also carry a meaning that is shared less directly.[4] They crystallise an intense, in-depth search for what creates sense and sensation, for what speaks to us as an act of culture and moves us as a body *at the same time.*

1   Re. the inspiration for their research, they name a German text by Martin Steinmann, "Sinnliche Dichte – Die neue Bedeutung eines alten Haustyps", in: *Werk, Bauen + Wohnen,* No. 10, 2002, p. 64–69.
2   Re. vertical access as a key element of utilisation, Timothée Giorgis and Juan Rodriguez often refer to the school projects by Herman Hertzberger, especially the Apollo schools in Amsterdam, 1980–1983.
3   Josef Frank, "Das Haus als Weg und Platz", *Der Baumeister,* No. 8, 1931, p. 316–323.
4   "Consensual reflex: A reflex created simultaneously in the affected organs if only one of them is stimulated", https://www.cnrtl.fr/definition/consensuel [trans.] (last accessed: February 8, 2023).

HAUS IN DEN BERGEN, LEYSIN / MOUNTAIN HOUSE, LEYSIN

Die im waadtländischen Alpenvorland gelegene Alm Pra Réaz öffnet sich zum Chablais hin, bietet weite Fernblicke und profitiert von reichlich Sonneneinstrahlung. Nur einige alte Landwirtschaftsgebäude stehen auf dieser Insel des Friedens, deren Leben sich dem Rhythmus der Jahreszeiten anpasst.

Der Entwurf kommt dem Wunsch nach, einen Neubau an diesem Ort zu integrieren, der seit einem Jahrhundert nicht verändert wurde. Dieses kleine Haus, dem eine kulturelle und morphologische Untersuchung des hier vorherrschenden Geistes vorausgegangen ist, versucht, eine soziale und nutzungstechnische Verbindung zur Lebensweise in einem Gebäude im waadtländischen Alpenvorland herzustellen. Der Grundriss ist eine Neuinterpretation der in dieser Region verbreiteten Typologie, bei der sich im tiefer liegenden Geschoss der Stall und in der Etage darüber zwei Zimmer gleicher Grösse befinden.

Das auf einem Felsvorsprung errichtete kompakte Haus wird durch ein zentrales tragendes Element, das dem Dachfirst entsprechend verläuft, in zwei Bereiche unterteilt: Im südöstlichen Teil befinden sich die Nutzräume (Esszimmer, Haupträume) und im nordwestlichen Teil sind die Serviceräume (Küche, Bäder, Erschliessung) untergebracht. Der im Nordwesten gelegene Bereich gliedert sich in zwei alkovenartige Teilräume auf, die sich durch grosse Schiebetüren zum Gang hin öffnen lassen.

Die Ansiedlung des Baukörpers und die Positionierung der Öffnungen sind Resultat der Reflexion über die Ausrichtung und das Verhältnis von Haus und Umgebung. Die unterschiedlich grossen Fenster setzen die Landschaft in Szene und verleihen jedem Raum einen ganz eigenen Charakter.

Located on the foothills of the Vaud Alps, the Pra Réaz mountain pasture opens onto the Chablais region, offering distant views and generous sunshine. Only a few old farm buildings occupy this haven of peace that still lives to the rhythm of the seasons.

The project responds to the request to integrate a new construction in this place that has remained intact for a century. Based on a cultural and morphological analysis of the spirit of the place, this small house seeks to establish a social and usage connection to the way of life of a mountain building on the foothills of the Vaud Alps. The plan reinterprets the dominant typology of this region, with the stable on the lower level and two rooms of the same dimensions on the upper level.

Standing on a headland, the house is compact and organised in two sections either side of a central load-bearing element corresponding to the ridge. The south-eastern part contains the serviced spaces (living room, main bedrooms) and the north-west part the serving spaces (kitchen, bathrooms, distribution). The north-western section is subdivided into alcove-type sub-spaces opening onto the corridor through large sliding doors.

The layout of the volume and the position of the openings contribute to the reflection on the framing and the relationship between the house and the site. The different sizes of the openings stage the landscape and give each of the rooms a particular character.

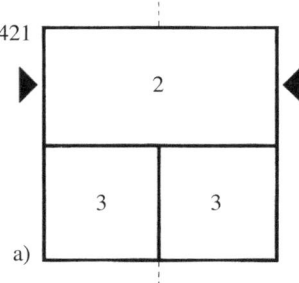

421 Grundrissschema der ersten Etage der Wohnhäuser, deren Küche sich auf der Rückseite befindet:
a) Der häufigste Grundrisstyp weist zwei identische Zimmer auf der Fassadenseite auf.
Daniel Glauser / Denise Raymond, *Les Maisons rurales du Canton de Vaud*, Bd. 2: Préalpes, Chablais, Lavaux, S. 223: Les grandes familles typologiques, Basel 2002.

**421 Schematic plan of the first floor of the residential buildings with the kitchen at the rear:
a) The most common floor plan type has two identical rooms on the façade side.
Daniel Glauser / Denise Raymond: *Les Maisons rurales du Canton de Vaud*, vol. 2: Préalpes, Chablais, Lavaux, p. 223: Les grandes familles typologiques, Basel 2002.**

Realisierung: 2009–2010
Bauherrschaft: Privat

**Completion: 2009–2010
Client: Private**

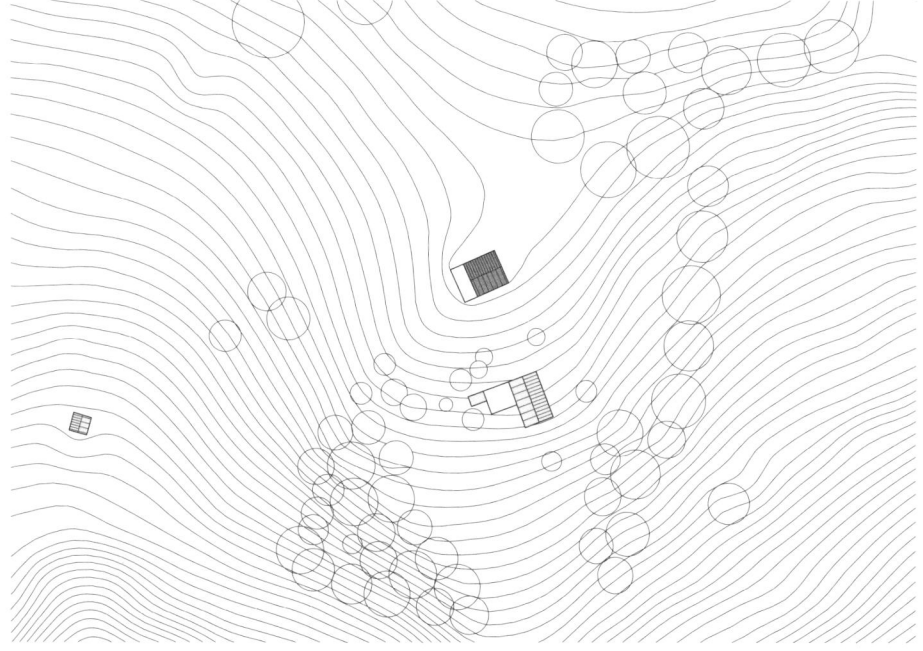

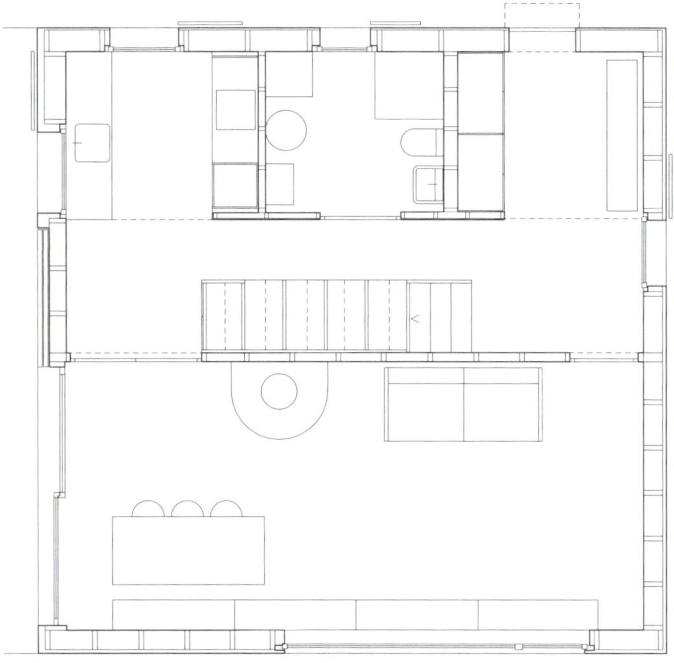
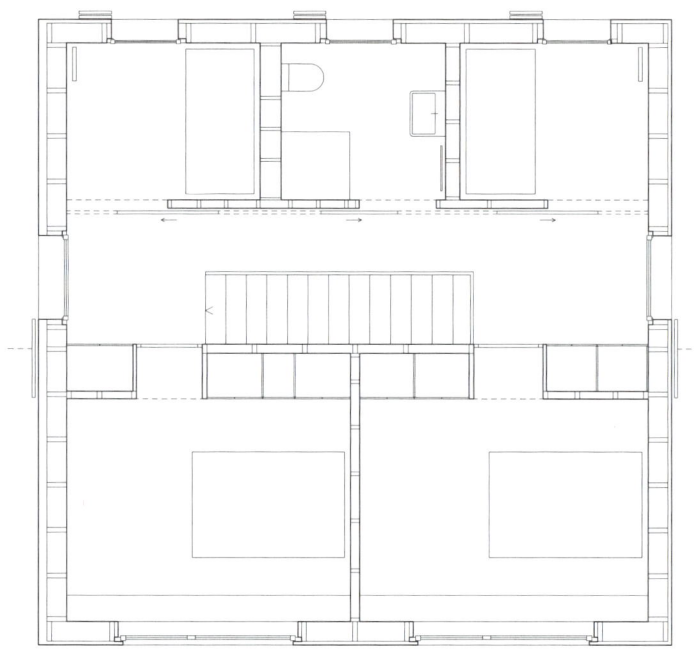

3 m

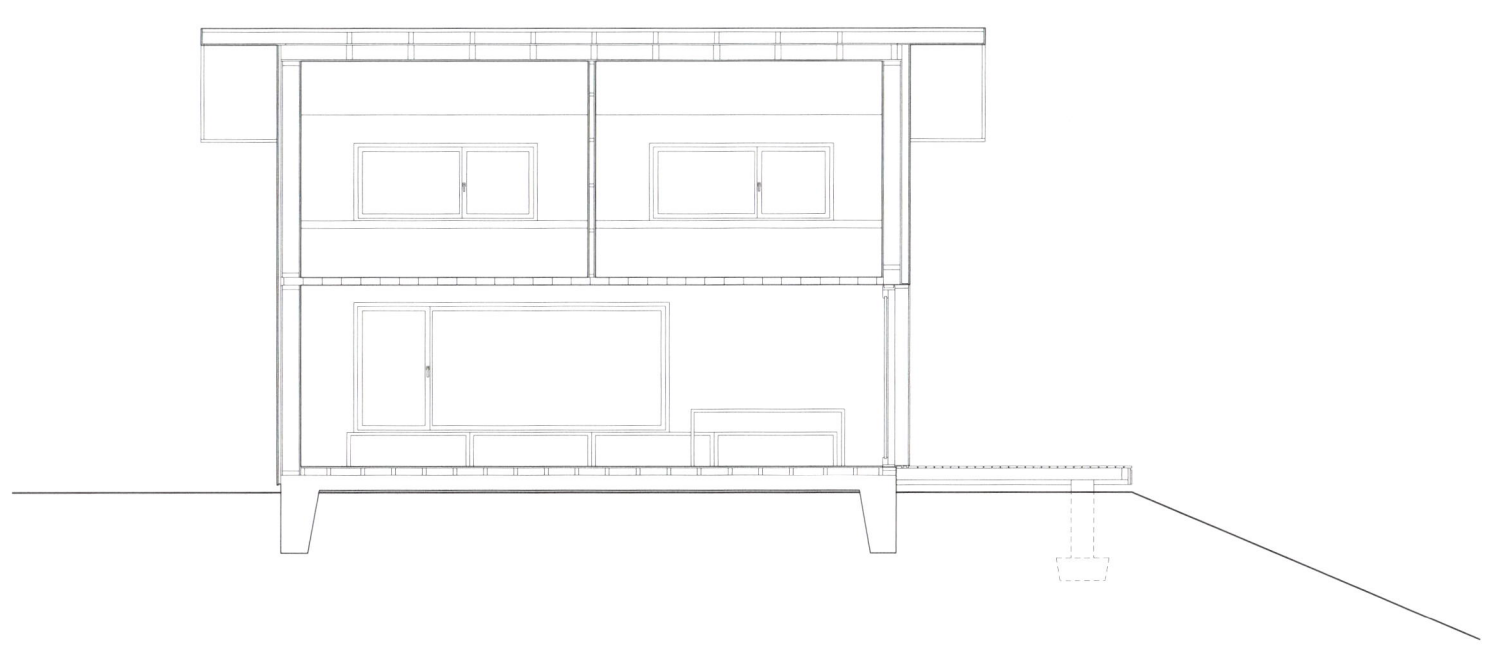

19

KINDERHEIM UTTINS, YVERDON-LES-BAINS

UTTINS CHILDREN'S HOME, YVERDON-LES-BAINS

Diese als grosses Einfamilienhaus konzipierte Notunterkunft für zehn Kinder befindet sich in einer Grünanlage. Dank der im Verhältnis zur Avenue de Grandson – der Hauptzugangsstrasse vom Norden des Kantons Waadt – zurückversetzten Lage konnte ein Eingangsbereich geschaffen werden, der den Mittelteil und die beiden Seitentrakte verbindet. Dieses vor Ort bereits existierende Prinzip erzeugt zwischen den Häusern an der Strassenfront und den weiter zurückversetzten eine logische, iterative Abfolge von Baukörpern und Freiflächen.

Die Gebäudegliederung ergab sich aufgrund eines besonders schützenswerten Baumbestands. Das dreiteilige Ensemble nimmt durch seine Gliederung die Proportionen der umliegenden Häuser auf. Im ersten Baukörper ist im Erdgeschoss die Verwaltung untergebracht, im zweiten die Küche und im dritten befinden sich Gemeinschaftsräume. Die erste Etage der beiden Flügel zu beiden Seiten des zentralen Baukörpers nimmt jeweils fünf Heimzimmer auf. Durch die versetzte Anordnung der drei Gebäudeteile sind Höfe entstanden, die eine Beziehung zwischen dem Haus und dem Garten herstellen.

Dank der Unterteilung des Gesamtvolumens wurden die räumlichen Beziehungen verstärkt und sind helle und freundliche Erschliessungsräume entstanden. Die Küche ist in der Mitte des Grundrisses angesiedelt und bildet eine Art Bindeglied zwischen Haupthof und Eingang. Die Grösse der Fenster und die materielle Umsetzung verleihen dem Baukörper die Anmutung eines Wohngebäudes. Die tragenden Fassadenwände wurden aus getöntem gestocktem Beton realisiert, wodurch das Erscheinungsbild eines Stampflehmbaus evoziert wird. Die Fensteröffnungen sind durch Fertigbetonrahmungen hervorgehoben, die direkt in den Verschalungen montiert wurden.

Designed as a large house, this emergency home for ten children is set in a long garden. The recessed position off Avenue de Grandson – the main access road from the north of the Canton of Vaud – makes it possible to develop a common entrance space with the two side houses. This principle, which already exists upstream on this avenue, enables the definition of a logical sequence of full and empty spaces that alternate between the houses facing the street and those that are recessed.

The structured form of the building derives from the preservation of some remarkable trees. The tripartite ensemble recaptures the proportions of the surrounding houses through this fragmentation. On the ground floor, the first volume features the administrative functions, the second the kitchen and the third the common spaces. On the first floor, two groups of five rooms are organised on either side of the central volume. The juxtaposition of three staggered volumes defines courtyards linking the house with the garden.

The division of the volume amplifies the spatial relationships and generates luminous and convivial distribution spaces. The kitchen is placed at the centre of the plan, in relation to the main courtyard and the entrance. The dimensions of the windows and the markings add to the expression of a residential construction. The load-bearing façades are made of tinted, bush-hammered concrete, reminiscent a rammed-clay building. The openings are marked by prefabricated concrete frames, which are mounted directly in the formwork.

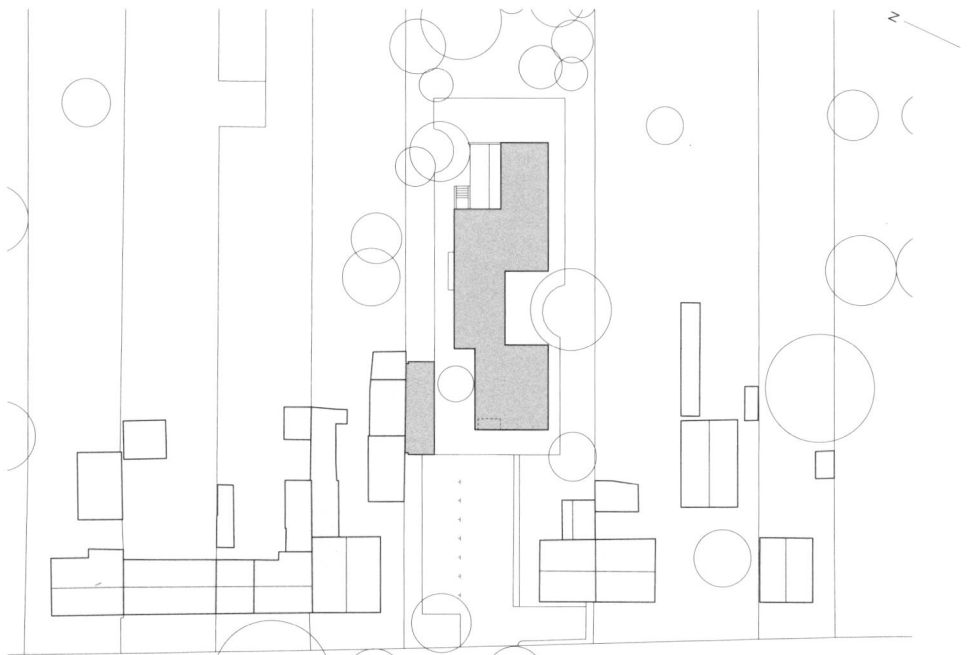

Realisierung: 2010–2015
Bauherrschaft: Fondation La Rambarde
Team: Carlo Piffaretti (Projektleitung und Bauleitung), Valeriya Todorova
Tragwerk: 2M ingénierie civile SA
Fachplanung: Olivier Zahn & Associés Sàrl (Heizung und Belüftung), Weinmann-Énergies SA (Sanitär), MAB-Ingénierie SA (Elektrik), EcoAcoustique SA (Akustik)

Construction: 2010–2015
Client: Fondation La Rambarde
Team: Carlo Piffaretti (Project and Construction Manager), Valeriya Todorova
Civil engineer: 2M ingénierie civile SA
Specialist engineers: Olivier Zahn & Associés Sàrl (heating and ventilation), Weinmann-Énergies SA (sanitary), MAB-Ingénierie SA (electrics), EcoAcoustique SA (acoustics)

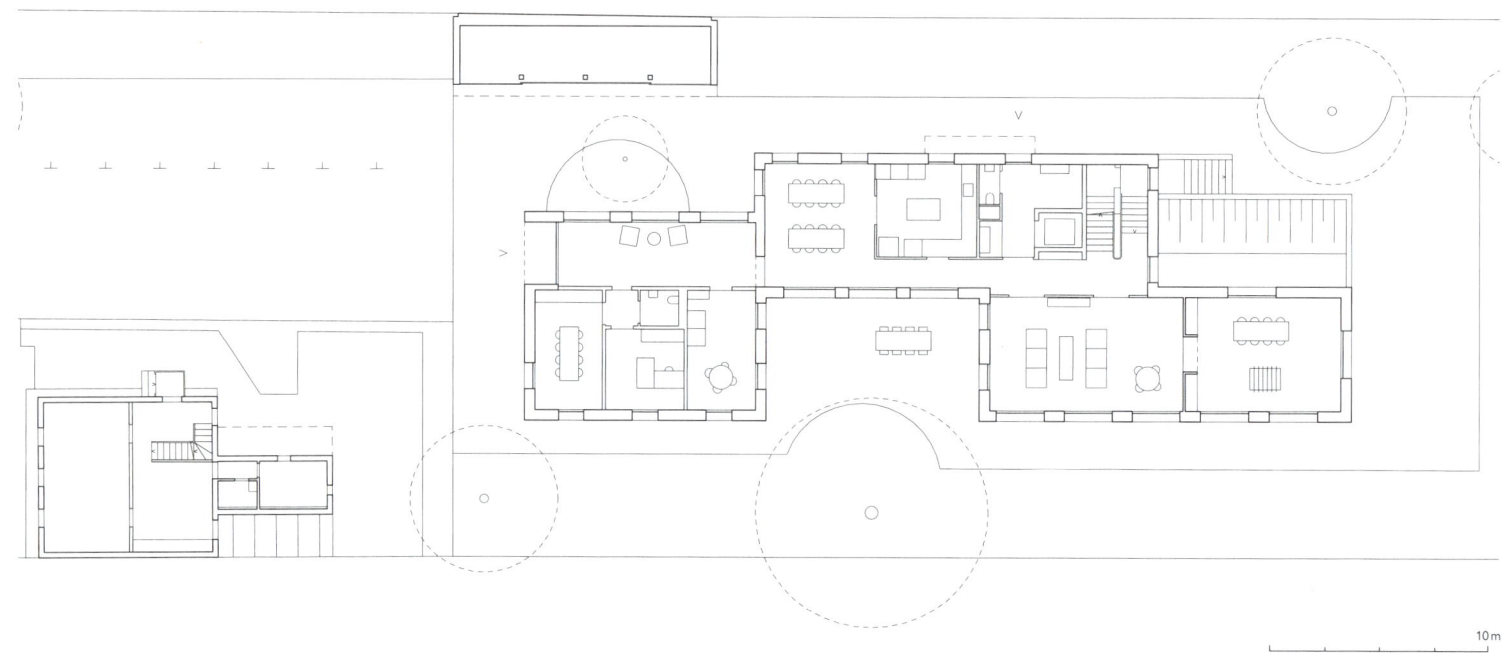

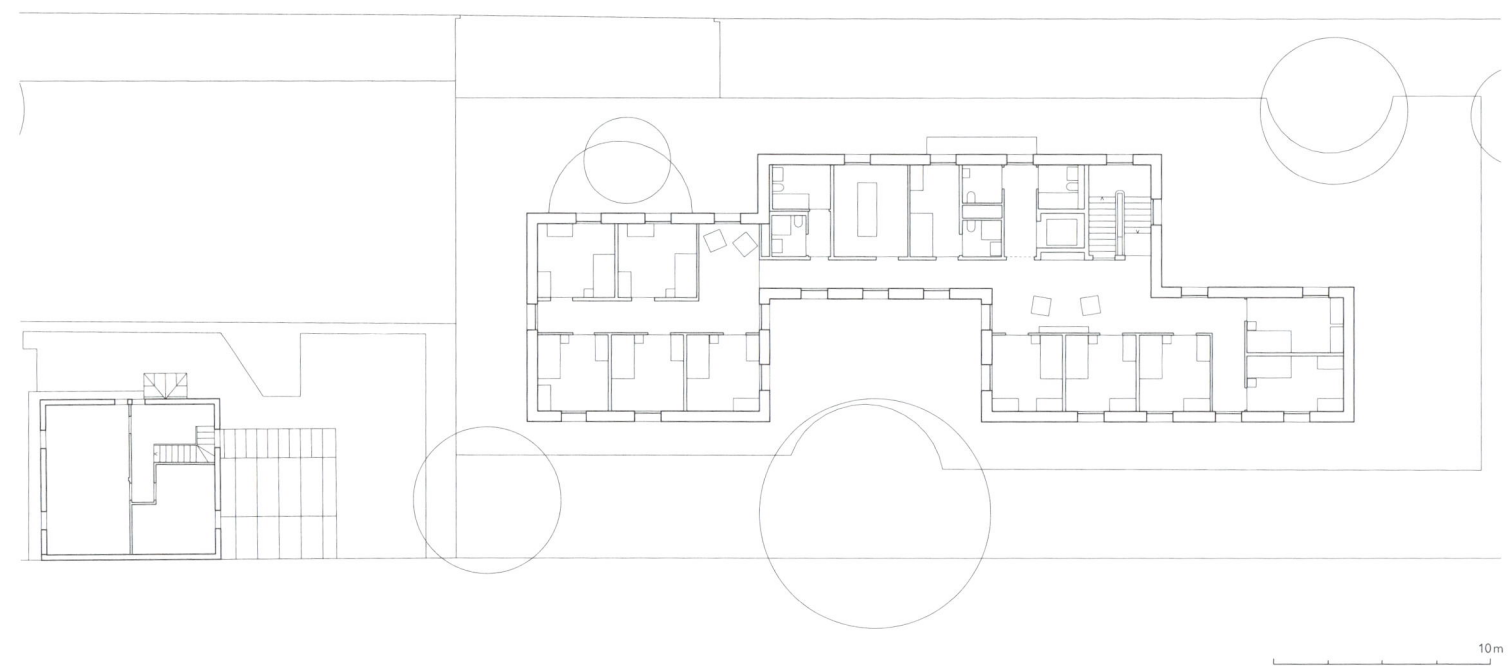

ERWEITERUNG KOMPLEX MIT SCHULE UND RATHAUS, SATIGNY

SCHOOL AND TOWN HALL COMPLEX EXTENSION, SATIGNY

Die grösste Schweizer Weinbaugemeinde Satigny beherbergt drei wichtige Gewerbegebiete des Kantons Genf und erfreut sich eines beträchtlichen Bevölkerungswachstums. Deren Entwicklung verlangt nach einer Wiederherstellung des Gleichgewichts mit ihrem dörflichen, historischen und landschaftlichen Umfeld.

Durch die Ansiedlung des neuen Gemeindesaals gegenüber der bereits bestehenden Sporthalle entsteht der Festplatz des Dorfes. Eine niedrige, halb ins Erdreich eingelassene Konstruktion verbindet den existierenden Gemeindebau mit seiner Erweiterung, sodass der Fernblick auf die Weinberge und die Berge des Jura erhalten bleibt. Das Rathaus wurde unter Wahrung seiner historischen Charakteristika umgebaut und saniert, wobei die gesamten Räumlichkeiten neu geordnet wurden und wichtige neue Räume entstanden sind.

Das Gebäude mit Gemeindesaal setzt sich entsprechend seines terrassenförmigen Profils, das man aus dem Weinbau nur allzu gut kennt, aus drei Teilen zusammen: Serviceräume, in den Obergeschossen Klassenräume, Hauptsaal und Bühne. Der Akzent liegt bei dem hauptsächlich in Holz errichteten Gebäude auf dem offenen Gebälk des Gemeindesaals – trapezförmige Kassetten aus Brettschichtholz.

Der Entwurf für das Schulgebäude weist vier rund um eine zentrale Halle angeordnete Baukörper auf und spiegelt so die volumetrische Ballungssituation wider, die für diverse Dörfer der Region Mandement charakteristisch ist. Der Grundriss ist so aufgeteilt, dass immer zwei bis drei Klassenräume um einen Garderobenbereich gruppiert sind. Diese Unterteilung fördert das Zugehörigkeitsgefühl und erleichtert die Orientierung der Schülerschaft im Gebäude.

Satigny is the largest wine-growing district in Switzerland, home to three major industrial zones in the Canton of Geneva, and is enjoying vigorous demographic growth. Its development requires a balance with its village, historical and landscape context.

The location of the new community hall in relation to the existing sports hall defines the village square. A low, semi-subterranean construction connects the existing community complex to its extension to preserve the distant view of the wine-growing hillsides and the Jura mountains. The town hall is transformed and renovated in a way that respects its historical features, while re-organising the premises as a whole and providing significant new spaces.

The community hall building comprises three parts based on a terraced profile, a familiar theme in the world of wine: the services, with classrooms on the upper floors, the main hall, and the stage. Built mainly of wood, the emphasis is on the visible framework of the community hall, made of trapezoidal, glued, laminated wood caissons.

The school project features a building fragmented into four volumes juxtaposed around a central hall, highlighting the scale of the volumetric agglomerations, as is characteristic of several hamlets in the Mandement region. The fragmented plan groups two to three classrooms around a cloakroom area; this sub-scale facilitates the sense of belonging and guides the pupils within the building.

Wettbewerb: 2010, 1. Preis
Etappe 1 (E1): 2016–2018
Etappe 2 (E2): 2019–2021
Etappe 3 (E3): 2022– (laufend)
Bauherrschaft: Gemeinde Satigny
Wettbewerbsteam: Carlo Piffaretti
Team E1: Frédéric Bravard (Projektleitung), Carlo Piffaretti, Valeriya Todorova, Sven Hiestand;
E2: Frédéric Bravard (Projektleitung und Bauleitung), Egzon Goçi, Alexandre Delencre, Théo Richard, Miguel Fernandes; E3: Alvise Allegretto und Martial Buisson (Co-Leitung Projekt und Bau), Alexandre Delencre, Estelle Delavy, Sven Grams
Bauleitung E1: Regtec SA; E2 und E3: Giorgis Rodriguez Architectes
Tragwerk E1 und E2: AB ingénieurs SA; E3: edms SA, Ratio Bois Sàrl und 102,2mètres Sàrl
Fachplanung: Conti & Associés ingénieurs SA (Heizung und Belüftung), Pierre Buclin SA (Sanitär E1 und E2), srg-engineering (Elektrik und Brandschutz E1 und E2; Sanitär und Elektrik E3), AcouConsult Sàrl (Akustik E1 und E2), AcouConsult Sàrl und BATJ SA (Akustik E3), BCS SA (Fassadenplanung E1), Orqual SA (Brandschutz E3)
Landschaftsarchitektur E1: Hüsler & Associés SA; E2: MAP Monnier Architecture du Paysage SA;
E3: Oxalis Architectes Paysagistes Associés Sàrl

Competition: 2010, 1st Prize
Stage 1 (S1): 2016–2018
Stage 2 (S2): 2019–2021
Stage 3 (S3): 2022– (ongoing)
Client:
Municipality of Satigny
Competition team: Carlo Piffaretti
Team, S1: Frédéric Bravard (Project Manager), Carlo Piffaretti, Valeriya Todorova, Sven Hiestand; S2: Frédéric Bravard (Project and Construction Manager), Egzon Goçi, Alexandre Delencre, Théo Richard, Miguel Fernandes; S3: Alvise Allegretto and Martial Buisson (Co-management project and construction), Alexandre Delencre, Estelle Delavy, Sven Grams
Building management:
S1: Regtec SA; S2 and S3:
Giorgis Rodriguez Architectes
Civil engineer: S1 and S2:
AB ingénieurs SA; S3: edms SA, Ratio Bois Sàrl and 102,2mètres Sàrl
Specialist engineers:
Conti & Associés ingénieurs SA (heating and ventilation),
Pierre Buclin SA (sanitary S1 and S2), srg-engineering (electrics and fire safety S1 and S2, sanitary and electrics S3), AcouConsult Sàrl (acoustics S1 and S2), AcouConsult Sàrl and BATJ SA (acoustics S3), BCS SA (façade S1), Orqual SA (fire safety S3)
Landscape architecture,
S1: Hüsler & Associés SA; S2:
MAP Monnier Architecture du Paysage SA; S3: Oxalis Architectes Paysagistes Associés Sàrl

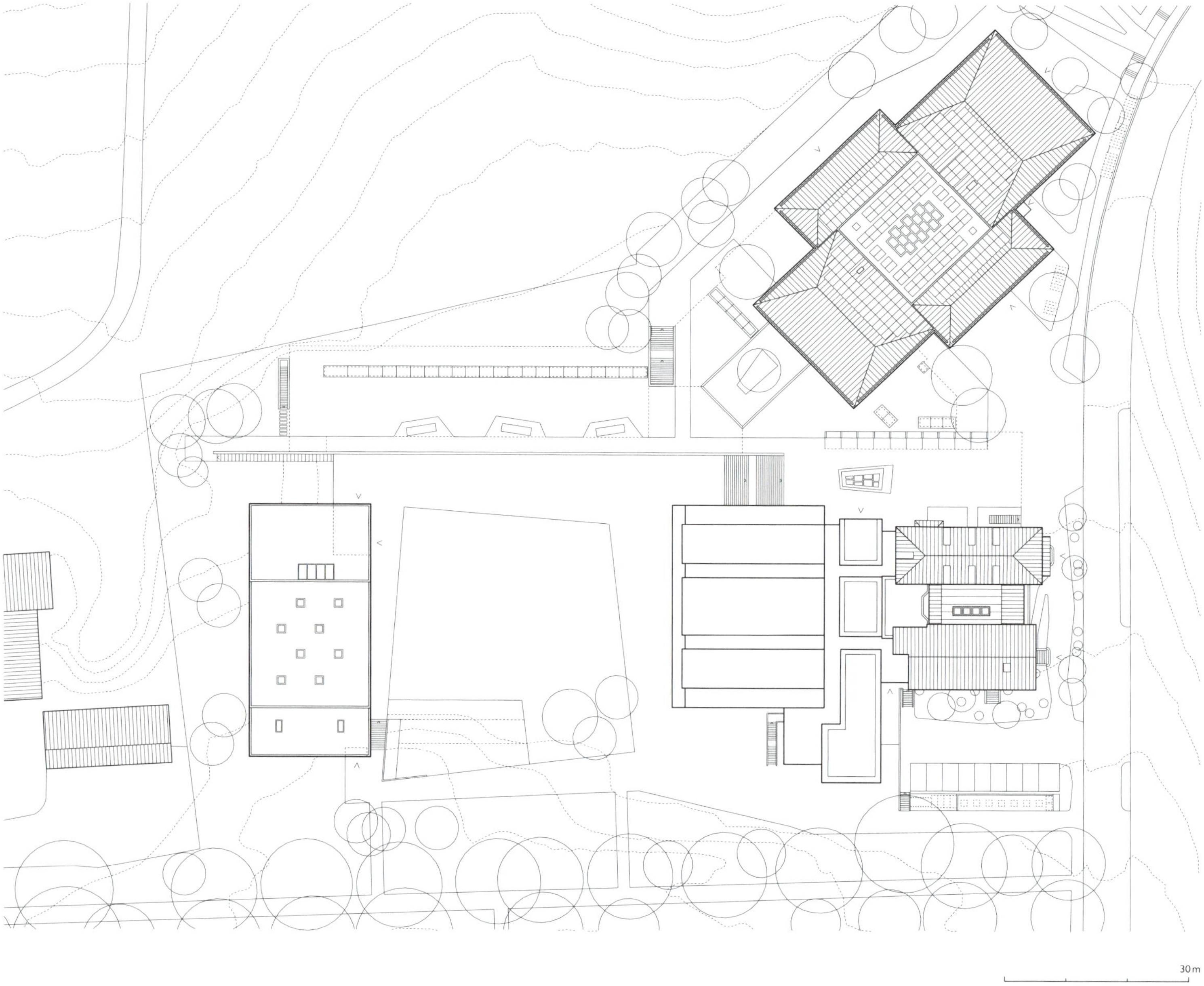

28

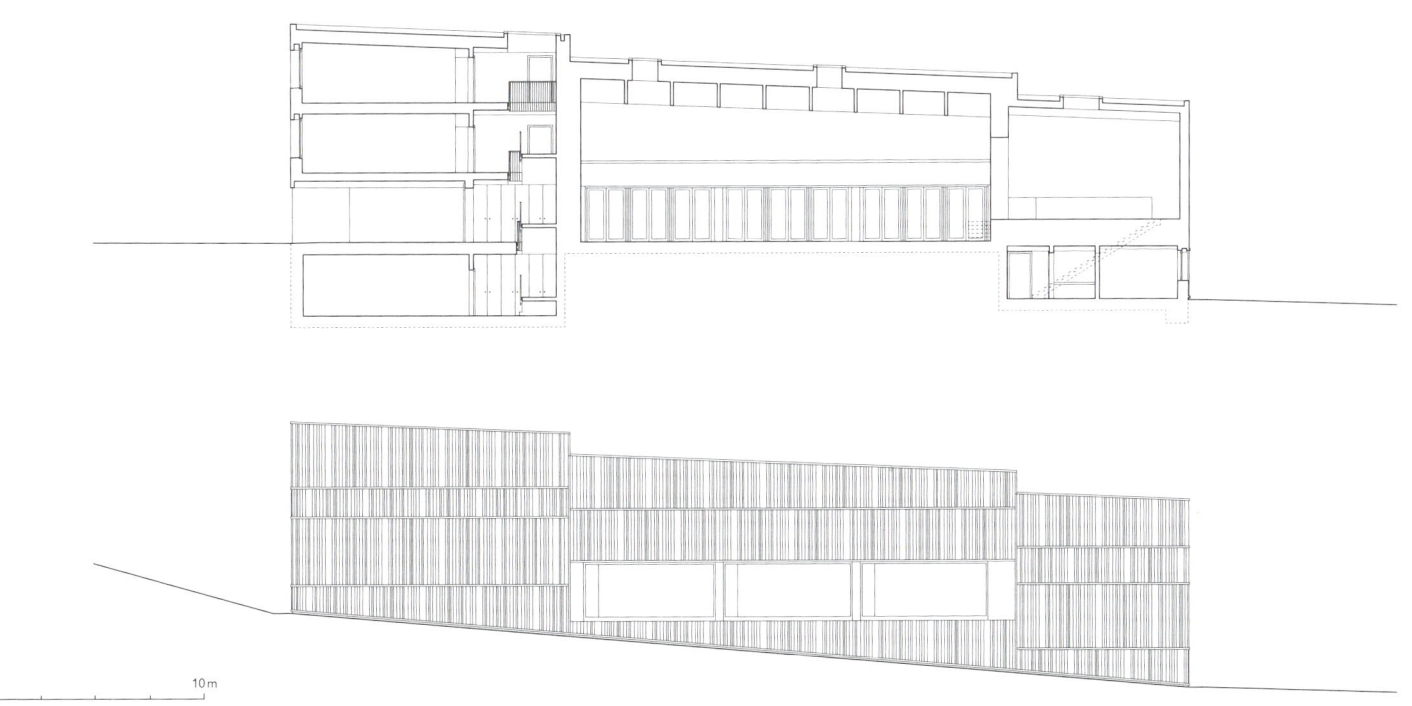

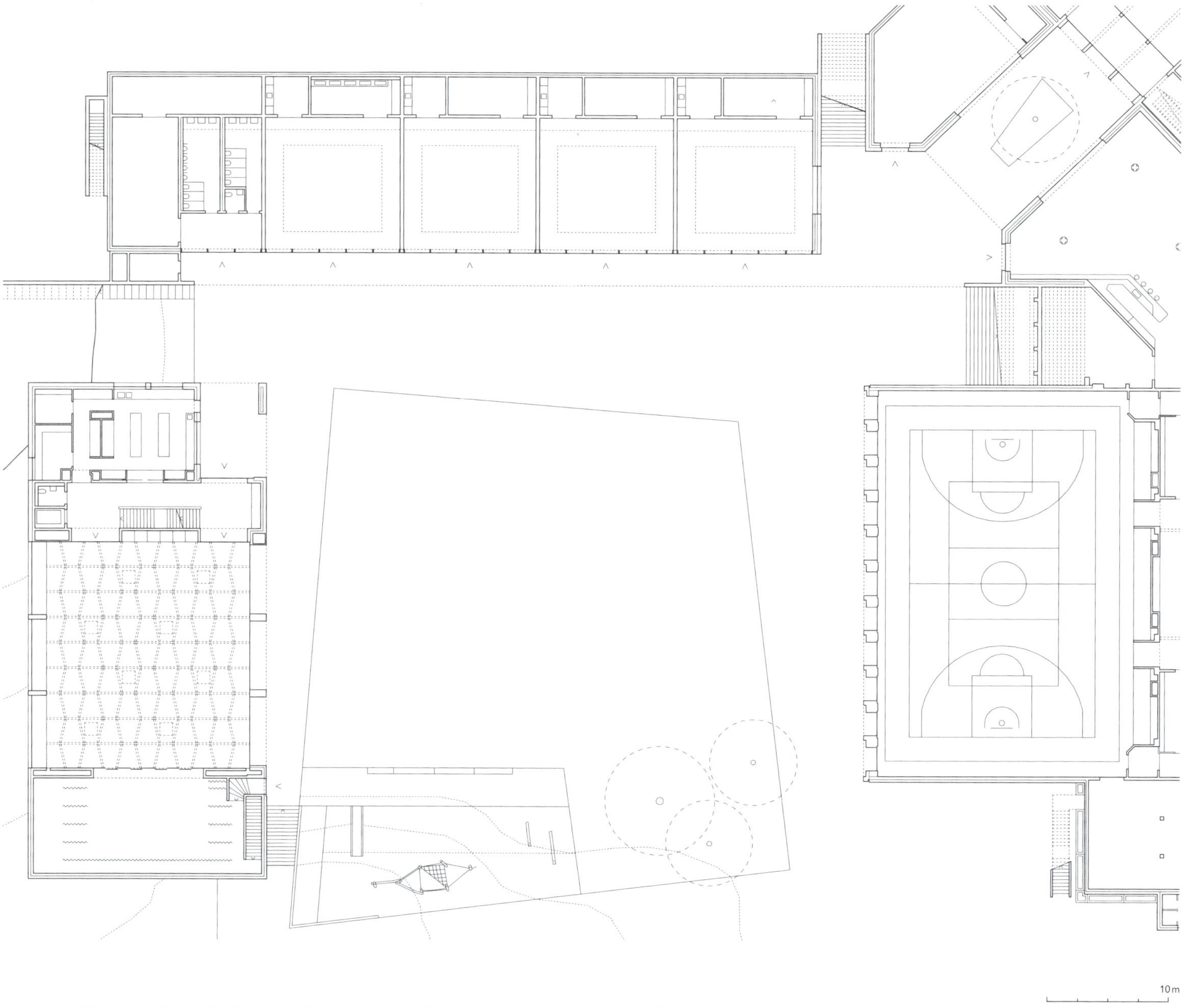

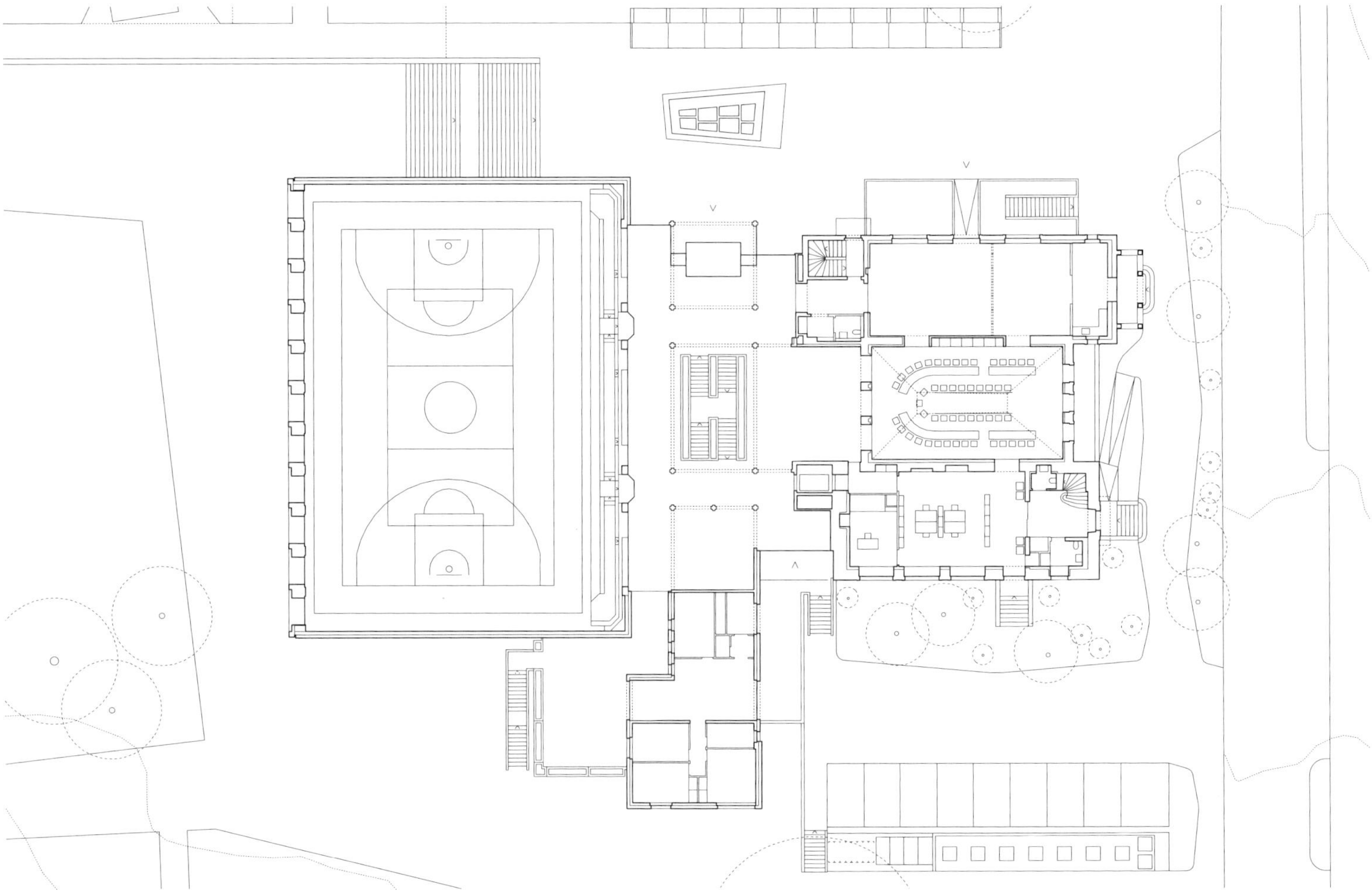

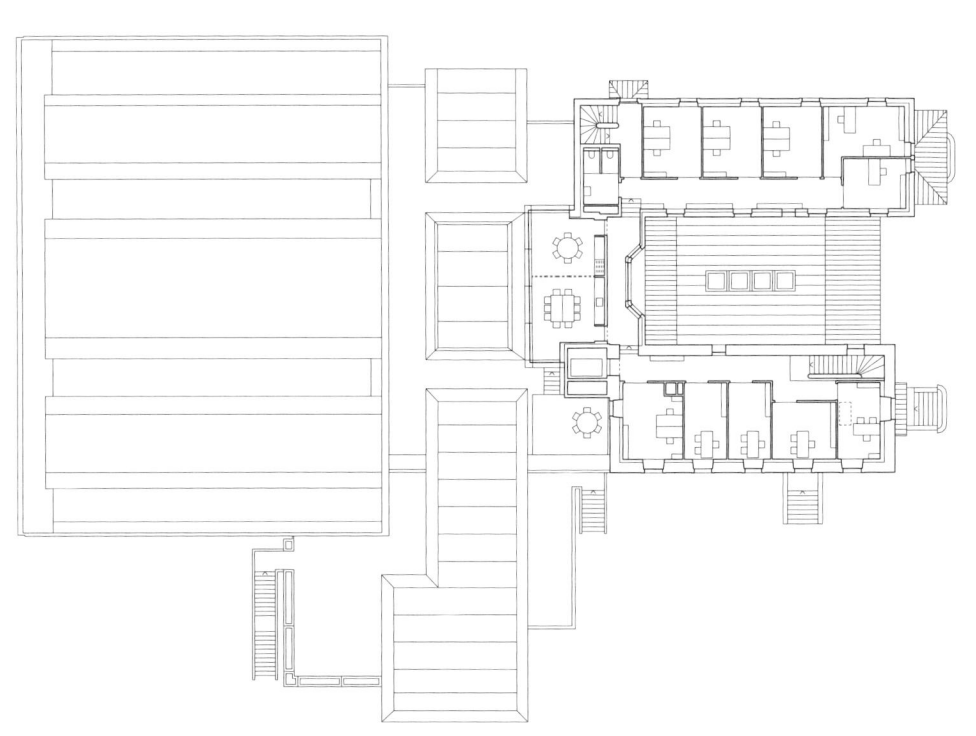

34

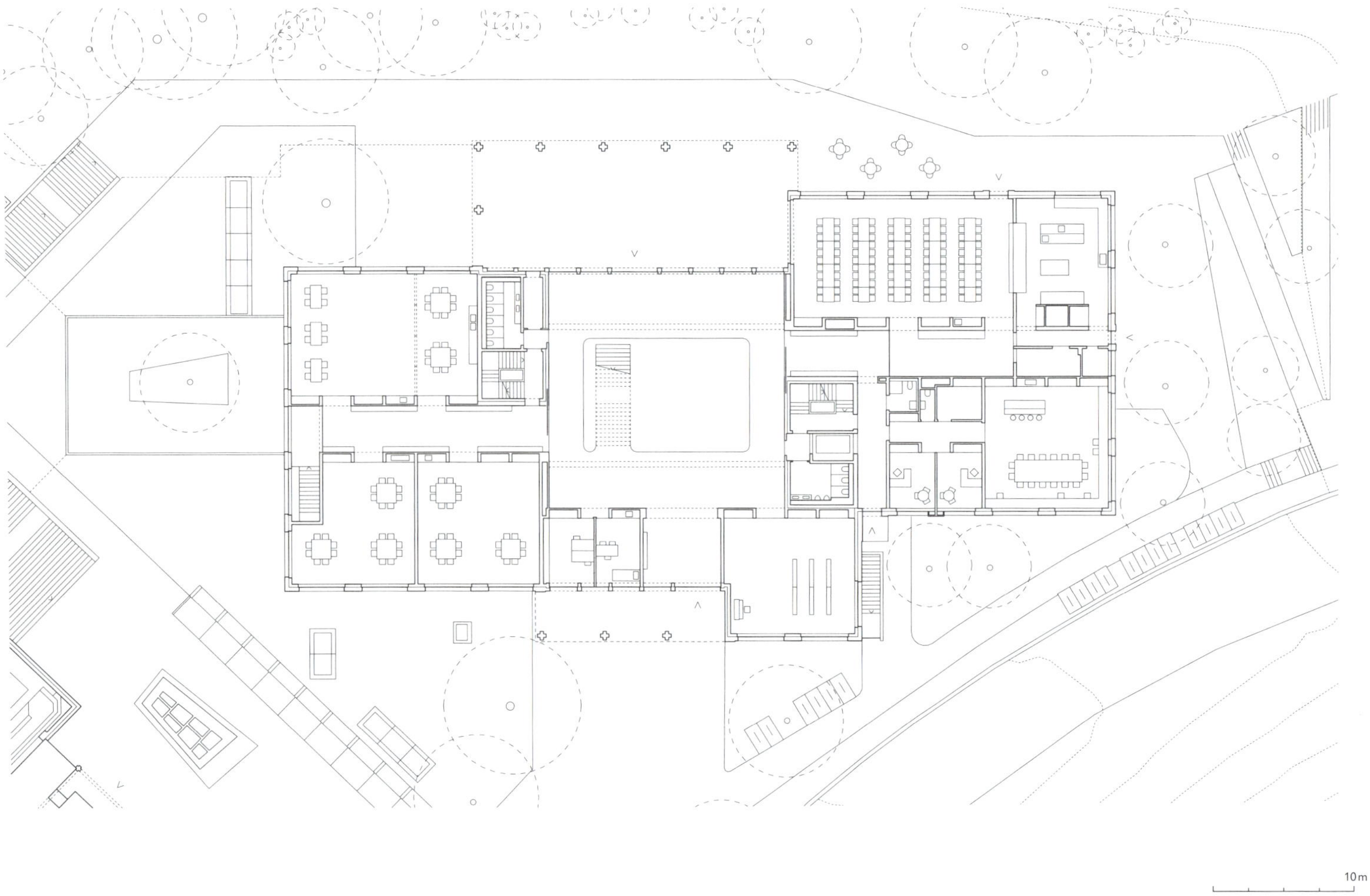

36

QUART

HIGHLIGHTS

2023 /2

www.quart.ch

Einzelausgabe / Individual edition

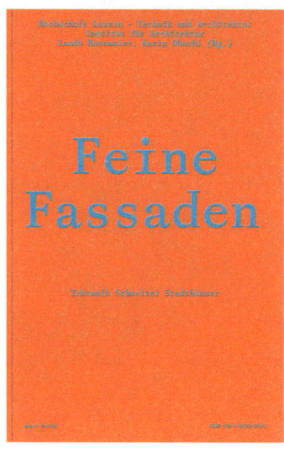

Feine Fassaden
Tektonik Schweizer Stadthäuser

Form und Widerstand bilden die Essenz aller architektonischer Arbeit. Besonders offensichtlich lässt sich das Wechselspiel von Wirkung und Machart an Fassaden ablesen. Sie orchestrieren den Übergang zwischen Innen und Aussen, sie zeitigen die zugrundeliegende Haltung, wie sich Bauwerke zur Umgebung verhalten. In ihrer Artikulation von Technik und Ästhetik, Tragen und Lasten, Proportion und Zweckmässigkeit sowie Rhythmik und Materialität sind sie zugleich Spiegel wechselnder Produktionsverfahren und gesellschaftlicher Wertesysteme.

Architekt Lando Rossmaier untersuchte mit Studierenden der Hochschule Luzern die Bandbreite architektonischer Konstruktions- und Ausdrucksmöglichkeiten von Schweizer Stadthausfassaden. Mit der vorliegenden Anthologie stellt er eine Auswahl von 86 Bauten des 20. Jahrhunderts und bis heute zur Verfügung, die in ihrer Tektonik feinfühlig gearbeitet wurden und dem urbanen Lebensgefühl seit Jahrzehnten Hintergrund sind.

Herausgegeben von:
Lando Rossmaier, Karin Ohashi

244 Seiten, 20,6 × 32 cm
101 Abbildungen,
86 Axonometrien
Hardcover, fadengeheftet
deutsch ISBN 978-3-03761-278-1
CHF 68.– / EUR 62,–

Feine Fassaden
Tektonik Schweizer Stadthäuser

Form and resistance are the essence of all architectural work. This is especially clear in the interaction between the effect and construction method of façades. They orchestrate the transition between interior and exterior worlds; they manifest the underlying approach and the way buildings behave towards their surroundings. In their articulation of engineering and aesthetics, supporting and loads, proportion and practicality, and rhythm and materiality, they reflect both varying production methods and social value systems.

The architect Lando Rossmaier worked with students at the University of Lucerne to study the range of architectural means of construction and expression with respect to Swiss townhouse façades. This anthology presents a selection of 86 buildings with sensitively developed tectonics, dating from the 20th century to the present day, all of which have formed a backdrop for an urban way of life for decades.

Edited by: Lando Rossmaier, Karin Ohashi

244 pages, 20.6 × 32 cm
101 images,
86 axonometric diagrams
Hardback, thread-stitched
German ISBN 978-3-03761-278-1
CHF 68.00 / EUR 62.00

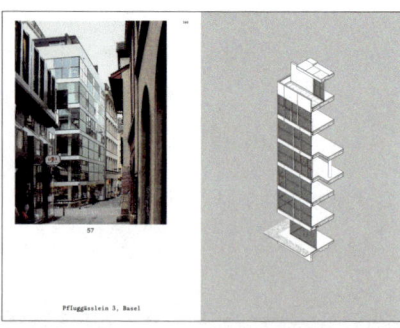

Pflugggässlein 3, Basel

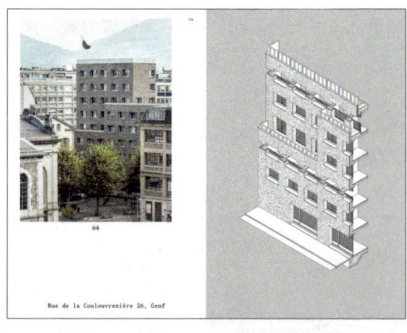

Rue de la Coulouvrenière 26, Genf

De aedibus international

27 DRDH – London/Antwerpen

Das sorgfältig und solide entwickelte Werk der Londoner Architekten Daniel Rosbottom und David Howarth ist seit 2000 kontinuierlich gewachsen. Jüngst wurden wichtige Bauten wie die ausergewöhnlich elegante und festliche Konzerthalle in Bodø (Norwegen) und die intelligent in die kleinstädtische Struktur verwobenen Alterswohnungen in Aarschot (Belgien) vollendet.

76 Seiten, 22,5 × 29 cm, 106 Abbildungen, 30 Pläne
fadengeheftete Broschur, CHF 48.– / EUR 44,–
deutsch/englisch ISBN 978-3-03761-129-6

The meticulously, carefully and solidly developed work by the London architects Daniel Rosbottom and David Howarth has continuously grown since 2000. Recent important buildings include the concert hall in Bodø (Norway), which has an outstandingly elegant and festive character, and the housing for the elderly in Aarschot, Belgium, which is intelligently integrated into the small-town structure.

76 pages, 22.5 × 29 cm, 106 images, 30 plans
Stitched brochure, CHF 48.00 / EUR 44.00
German/English ISBN 978-3-03761-129-6

28 Liebman Villavecchia – Barcelona

Eileen Joy Liebman und Fernando Villavecchia haben seit 1987 mit Sitz in Barcelona (Spanien) eine Reihe unterschiedlicher Projekte realisiert. Ihr Schwerpunkt liegt auf Wohnarchitektur und der Renovierung historischer Gebäude in den verschiedensten ländlichen und städtischen Umgebungen. Zu den Projekten zählen die sorgfältige Restaurierung und Umgestaltung der Casa Coderch Milá von 1958 in Cadaqués (2017) und die Casa Sant Llorenç (2014) in den Bergen von Lérida.

88 Seiten, 22,5 × 29 cm, 156 Abbildungen, 52 Pläne
fadengeheftete Broschur, CHF 48.– / EUR 44,–
deutsch/englisch, ISBN 978-3-03761-274-3

Since 1987, Eileen Joy Liebman and Fernando Villavecchia have produced a series of diverse projects from their studio in Barcelona, Spain, with an emphasis on residential architecture and the renovation of historic buildings in a range of rural and urban contexts. Projects include the careful restoration and adaptation of the 1958 Casa Coderch Milá in Cadaqués (2017) and the Casa Sant Llorenç (2014) in the mountains of Lérida.

88 pages, 22.5 × 29 cm, 156 images, 52 plans
Stitched brochure, CHF 48.00 / EUR 44.00
German/English ISBN 978-3-03761-274-3

29 Mikou Studio – Paris

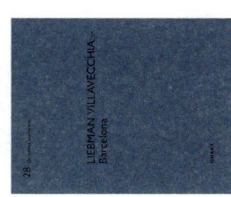

Die Zwillingsschwestern Selma Mikou und Salwa Mikou gründeten 2006 in Paris – nach langjähriger Mitarbeit bei Jean Nouvel und Renzo Piano – ihr eigenes Büro. Jedes Projekt bedeutet für sie vorerst, sich von vorgefassten Formen zu befreien, um originelle Lösungen zu schaffen, die die Dimension des emotionalen Raumerlebnisses in das Zentrum rücken. So sind zahlreiche prominente Bauten in Châteauroux (2021) entstanden, wie das als dynamische Figur entwickelte Balsanéo Aquatics Center.

76 Seiten, 22,5 × 29 cm, 119 Abbildungen, 49 Pläne
fadengeheftete Broschur, CHF 48.– / EUR 44,–
deutsch/englisch ISBN 978-3-03761-269-9

The twin sisters Selma Mikou and Salwa Mikou founded their own Paris office in 2006 – after working for many years for Jean Nouvel and Renzo Piano. Each project primarily aims to liberate itself from preconceived forms in order to create original solutions that focus on the dimension of an emotional spatial experience. The architects have produced numerous prominent buildings in this way, including the Balsanéo Aquatics Center in Châteauroux (2021).

76 pages, 22.5 × 29 cm, 119 images, 49 plans
Stitched brochure, CHF 48.00 / EUR 44.00
German/English ISBN 978-3-03761-269-9

30 One O One – Seoul/서울

Choi Wook ist Gründer und Protagonist des Büros One O One in Seoul, Südkorea. Seit 2000 entstehen hier Jahr für Jahr einige Preziosen der Baukunst, die deutliche Affinitäten ebenso zur koreanischen Architekturtradition wie zur europäischen Architektur aufweisen. Handwerkskunst, Präzision im Detail, Materialechtheit und eindrückliche Raumschöpfungen sind nur einige der bemerkenswerten Attribute der 13 hier vorgestellten Projekte.

180 Seiten, 22,5 × 29 cm, 168 Abbildungen, 32 Pläne
fadengeheftete Broschur, CHF 48.– / EUR 44,–
deutsch/englisch ISBN 978-3-03761-283-5
koreanisch/englisch ISBN 978-3-03761-284-2

Choi Wook is the founder and protagonist of the One O One office in Seoul, South Korea. Since 2000, he has been creating a number of architectural gems year after year that show clear affinities to Korean architectural traditions as well as to European architecture. Craftsmanship, precision in detail, material authenticity and impressive spatial creations are just some of the remarkable attributes of the 13 projects presented here.

180 pages, 22.5 × 29 cm, 168 images, 32 plans
Stitched brochure, CHF 48.00 / EUR 44.00
German/English ISBN 978-3-03761-283-5
Korean/English ISBN 978-3-03761-284-2

Architektur machen
Schweizer Architekturschaffende im Gespräch

In insgesamt acht Interviews mit Schweizer Architekten und Architektinnen wird der Entwurfsprozess erörtert. In den Gesprächen geht es um die Bedeutung, die Architektur für die Entwerfenden hat, wie an eine Aufgabe herangegangen wird, um den Wert des Bildes, den Umgang mit Gesetzen und darum, wie die Herausforderungen des Klimawandels gehandhabt werden. Die Texte geben spannende Einblicke in das Schaffen der Architekturschaffenden. Geführt wurden die Interviews mit Barbara Buser (Baubüro Insitu), Andreas Bründler (Buchner Bründler Architekten), Christian Kerez, Roger Boltshauser, Oliver Lütjens und Thomas Padmanabhan, Annette Gigon (Gigon Guyer), Steffen Hägele und Tina Küng (DU Studio) sowie Stefan Wülser. In den unterschiedlichen und teilweise gegensätzlichen Haltungen der Architekturschaffenden offenbart sich, was Architektur alles sein kann und wie viele verschiedene Zugänge sie hat.
Ergänzt werden die acht Interviews durch Abbildungen und Pläne, die spielerisch auf die thematisierte Architektur verweisen.

Architektur machen
Schweizer Architekturschaffende im Gespräch

Swiss architects discuss the design process in a total of eight interviews. The interviews focus on the importance of architecture for the designers, how a task is approached, the value of the image, how building laws are addressed and how the challenges of climate change are handled. The texts provide fascinating insights into the work of the architects. The interviews were conducted with Barbara Buser (Baubüro Insitu), Andreas Bründler (Buchner Bründler Architekten), Christian Kerez, Roger Boltshauser, Oliver Lütjens and Thomas Padmanabhan, Annette Gigon (Gigon Guyer), Steffen Hägele and Tina Küng (DU Studio) and Stefan Wülser. The different and sometimes contradictory attitudes of the architects reveal what architecture can be and how many different approaches there are.
The eight interviews are supplemented by illustrations and plans that playfully refer to the architecture discussed.

ARCHITEKTUR MACHEN
SCHWEIZER ARCHITEKTURSCHAFFENDE IM GESPRÄCH

ROGER BOLTSHAUSER
CHRISTIAN KEREZ
BUCHNER BRÜNDLER
BAUBÜRO INSITU
LÜTJENS PADMANABHAN
DETOUR UNIVERSE
GIGON GUYER
STEFAN WÜLSER

QUART

120 Seiten, 20 × 26 cm
57 Abbildungen, 10 Pläne
Leinenband, fadengeheftet
deutsch
ISBN 978-3-03761-282-8
CHF 48.– / EUR 48,–

120 pages, 20 × 26 cm
57 illustrations, 10 plans
Cloth-bound, thread-stitched
German
ISBN 978-3-03761-282-8
CHF 48.00 / EUR 48.00

Hotel Palace Luzern – Denkmalpflegerische Erneuerung
Iwan Bühler Architekten

1906 wurde das Hotel Palace an der prominenten Luzerner Quai-Promenade nach Plänen von Heinrich Meili-Wapf – einem der wichtigsten Luzerner Architekten jener Zeit – erstellt. Das wie aus einem Guss entstandene mächtige Gebäude wurde sowohl aufgrund seiner fortschrittlichen Bau- und Gebäudetechnik als auch wegen seiner architektonischen Gestaltung zu einem der in der Schweiz wichtigsten Hotelbauten seiner Zeit.
Nach mehreren zeittypischen Umbauten im Inneren wurde das Gebäude 2018–2022 durch den Luzerner Architekten Iwan Bühler einer umfassenden sorgfältigen denkmalpflegerischen Erneuerung unterzogen. Das Ergebnis zeichnet sich aus durch einen optimalen Erhalt der bestehenden Substanz, das Aufdecken und Wiederherstellen der vielmals differenzierten, feinsinnigen Qualitäten und des Reichtums des ursprünglichen Bauwerks sowie durch behutsame, nutzungsbedingte Erneuerungen einzelner Teile im und am Gebäude.

Hotel Palace Lucerne – Heritage Renovation
Iwan Bühler Architekten

In 1906, the Hotel Palace was built along Lucerne's prominent Quai Promenade according to plans by Heinrich Meili-Wapf – one of the most important Lucerne architects of the time. The mighty building, which appears as if it were developed out of a single block, is regarded as one of the most important Swiss hotel developments of its time, both due to its pioneering construction and building technology, and due to its architectural design.
After several interior conversions that were typical for the times of their implementation, the building was carefully and comprehensively renewed by the Lucerne-based architect Iwan Bühler between 2018 and 2022, taking aspects of monument preservation into account. This demanded ideally preserving the existing building fabric, while revealing and reproducing the building's often differentiated and subtle qualities, as well as the wealth of the original building. The work also included carefully renewing individual elements inside and outside the building to accommodate current utilisation.

Herausgegeben von:
Iwan Bühler
Textbeiträge: Iwan Bühler,
Cony Grünenfelder,
Peter Omachen u.a.

136 Seiten, 22,5 × 29 cm
135 Abbildungen, 31 Pläne
Leinenband, fadengeheftet
deutsch/englisch
ISBN 978-3-03761-267-5
CHF 68.– / EUR 62,–

Edited by: Iwan Bühler
Articles by: Iwan Bühler,
Cony Grünenfelder,
Peter Omachen et al.

136 pages, 22,5 × 29 cm
135 images, 31 plans
Cloth-bound, thread-stitched
German/English
ISBN 978-3-03761-267-5
CHF 68.00 / EUR 62.00

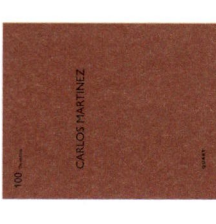

48 Tom Munz Architekt

Seit 2013 führt Tom Munz in St. Gallen sein Büro und hat eine Vielzahl überaus qualitätsvoller Bauten hervorgebracht, die sich allesamt durch sein besonderes Interesse am konstruktiven und tektonischen Ausdruck auszeichnen. Beispielhaft hierfür steht etwa das Wohnhaus Holzenstein in Romanshorn, dessen Gestalt der Moderne verpflichtet ist und das durch das Wechselspiel zwischen den dezent beige eingefärbten Betonflächen und den hölzernen Fensterelementen einen ausgesprochen poetischen Charakter entfaltet.

72 Seiten, 16,5 × 21 cm, 77 Abbildungen, 17 Pläne
fadengeheftete Broschur, CHF 28.– / EUR 25,–
deutsch/englisch ISBN 978-3-03761-273-6

Tom Munz established his St. Gallen office in 2013. Since then, he has produced a number of extremely high-quality buildings that are always developed with a special interest in structural and tectonic expression. For instance Wohnhaus Holzenstein in Romanshorn is a design inspired by Modernism, thriving on the interaction between reserved, beige-stained concrete wall surfaces and wooden window elements to achieve an extremely poetic radiance.

72 pages, 16.5 × 21 cm, 77 images, 17 plans
Stitched brochure, CHF 28.00 / EUR 25.00
German/English ISBN 978-3-03761-273-6

49 Javier Müller

Seit 2017 führt der spanische Architekt Javier Müller ein Büro in Genf. Sein Streben nach radikaler Reduktion manifestiert sich in einer zeitlosen Architektur, die ihr soziales Potenzial voll entfaltet. Mit subtilen Eingriffen und einem sparsamen Einsatz von Mitteln erzeugt er so eine ungekünstelte Architektur, deren Form sich ganz in den Dienst der Funktion und Lebensqualität ihrer Nutzerschaft stellt. Beispielhaft für eine solche Abstraktion durch Rationalisierung ist der Umbau des Doppelhauses B in Bernex.

52 Seiten, 16,5 × 21 cm, 39 Abbildungen, 9 Pläne
fadengeheftete Broschur, CHF 28.– / EUR 25,–
deutsch/englisch ISBN 978-3-03761-290-3

The Spanish architect Javier Müller has managed his office in Geneva since 2017. His striving for radical reduction is manifested in timeless architecture that fully exploits its social potential. Subtle measures and the economic application of means creates uncontrived architecture in which the form entirely serves the function and its users' quality of life. One example of such abstraction through rationalisation is the conversion of Duplex B in Bernex.

52 pages, 16.5 × 21 cm, 39 images, 9 plans
Stitched brochure, CHF 28.00 / EUR 25.00
German/English ISBN 978-3-03761-290-3

99 Stocker Lee

Die Schweizerin Melanie Stocker und der Südkoreaner Dong Joon Lee führen seit 2005 in Mendrisio ihr Studio d'architettura. Im Laufe der Zeit sind einige bemerkenswerte, sorgfältig entwickelte Bauten im Tessin und in Südkorea entstanden, so etwa das Mehrfamilienhaus Ca'Ospiti in Rancate, dessen Baukörper wie ein reduzierter Archetypus erscheint, der in seinem Innern fünf effizient angeordnete Wohnungen birgt; oder das ebenso stringent und minimalistisch gehaltene Wohn- und Geschäftshaus Godung in der Nähe von Seoul.

108 Seiten, 22,5 × 29 cm, 105 Abbildungen, 60 Pläne
fadengeheftete Broschur, CHF 48.– / EUR 44,–
deutsch/englisch ISBN 978-3-03761-286-6

The Swiss Melanie Stocker and the South Korean Dong Joon Lee have been running their Studio d'architettura in Mendrisio since 2005. Over time they have created some remarkable, carefully developed buildings in Ticino and South Korea, such as the Ca'Ospiti apartment building in Rancate, whose structure appears like a reduced archetype that houses five cleverly-nested flats inside; or the equally stringent and minimalist Godung residential and commercial building near Seoul.

108 pages, 22.5 × 29 cm, 105 images, 60 plans
Stitched brochure, CHF 48.00 / EUR 44.00
German/English ISBN 978-3-03761-286-6

100 Carlos Martinez

Seit über 30 Jahren führt Carlos Martinez in Berneck sein Architekturbüro. Bekannt geworden ist er durch den zusammen mit Pipilotti Rist entwickelten «roten Teppich von St. Gallen» – eine wundersame städtebauliche Intervention, die ein ehemals zerklüftetes Konglomerat von Restflächen und Verkehrsfunktionen zu einem homogenen, identitätsstiftenden Ganzen zusammenfasst. Mit viel Verve und in intensiver Auseinandersetzung mit dem städtebaulichen Kontext und dem Bestand sind in den letzten drei Dekaden zahlreiche architektonische Projekte entstanden.

144 Seiten, 22,5 × 29 cm, 160 Abbildungen, 77 Pläne
fadengeheftete Broschur, CHF 48.– / EUR 44,–
deutsch/englisch ISBN 978-3-03761-272-9

Carlos Martinez has been running his architectural office in Berneck for over 30 years. He made a name for himself through his collaboration with Pipilotti Rist entitled "red carpet of St. Gallen", a wonderful urban-planning intervention that brings together the formerly haphazard conglomerate of remnant spaces and transport functions. His great energy and inventive engagement with the urban-planning context and its existing structures have led to numerous architectural projects.

144 pages, 22.5 × 29 cm, 160 images, 77 plans
Stitched brochure, CHF 48.00 / EUR 44.00
German/English ISBN 978-3-03761-272-9

Monografie / Monograph

Peter Märkli. Everything one invents is true

Peter Märkli zählt seit den frühen 1980er-Jahren zweifellos zu den markantesten Deutschschweizer Architekten der ersten Stunde. Seine einprägsamen Bauten lassen sich jedoch nicht leicht in das Schema dieser Architekturbewegung einordnen. Zu sehr sind die einzelnen Bauwerke intensiv bearbeitete Individuen, die einer fortdauernden Bewegung des Suchens folgen. Immer eröffnen sie eigenständig und eindringlich Verbindungen der Geschichte der Architektur mit dem Impetus einer zeitüber-dauernden Gültigkeit.
Im vorliegenden Band sind 17 Bauten der letzten 15 Jahre mit Texten, Plänen und Abbildungen ausführlich dargestellt. Ergänzt wird die bemerkenswerte Werkdarstellung mit erhellenden Essays von Florian Beigel & Philip Christou, Franz Wanner und Ellis Woodman. Ein spannendes Interview mit Peter Märkli von Elena Markus und einzelne Statements des Architekten runden die eindrückliche Sammlung ab.
Herausgegeben von Pamela Johnston
Textbeiträge: Florian Beigel & Philip Christou, Pamela Johnston, Peter Märkli, Elena Markus, Franz Wanner, Ellis Woodman

Peter Märkli. Everything one invents is true

Since the early 1980s, Peter Märkli has been one of the most striking protagonists of German Swiss architecture from the earliest period of its emergence. However his impressive buildings cannot be easily classified in the scheme of this architectural movement, since the individual buildings are intensely developed individuals that follow the history of architecture in an independent, powerful way and express the impetus of timeless validity.
This volume presents 17 buildings in detail from the last 15 years with texts, plans and images. The remarkable presentation of works is complemented by enlightening essays by Florian Beigel & Philip Christou, Franz Wanner and Ellis Woodman. An exciting interview with Peter Märkli by Elena Markus and individual statements by the architects round off the impressive collection.
Edited by: Pamela Johnston
Articles by: Florian Beigel & Philip Christou, Pamela Johnston, Peter Märkli, Elena Markus, Franz Wanner, Ellis Woodman

240 Seiten, 29 × 29 cm
178 Abbildungen, 75 Pläne,
101 Zeichnungen
Hardcover, fadengeheftet
CHF 138.– / EUR 126,–
englisch ISBN 978-3-03761-138-8
(eingelegtes Booklet deutsch)
englisch ISBN 978-3-03761-139-5
(eingelegtes Booklet japanisch)

240 pages, 29 × 29 cm
178 illustrations, 75 plans,
101 sketches
Hardback, stitched
CHF 138.00 / EUR 126.00
English ISBN 978-3-03761-138-8
(German in an inserted booklet)
English ISBN 978-3-03761-139-5
(Japanese in an inserted booklet)

Gion A. Caminada – Cul zuffel e l'aura dado

Von Gion A. Caminada ist in der bündnerischen Surselva ein architektonisches Werk entstanden, das wie kein anderes unmittelbar in den ökonomischen, geografischen und bautechnischen Prämissen eines Ortes und den Lebensgewohnheiten seiner Bevölkerung bedingt ist.
Die neue Buchausgabe umfasst die Texte und die Projektsammlung des Bandes Cul zuffel e l'aura dado und ist erweitert um eine Auswahl der neueren Projekte seit 2005.
Herausgegeben von: Bettina Schlorhaufer
Fotos: Lucia Degonda
Textbeiträge: Gion A. Caminada, Jürg Conzett, Bettina Schlorhaufer, Peter Schmid, Martin Tschanz, Peter Rieder, Walter Zschokke

Gion A. Caminada – Cul zuffel e l'aura

Gion A. Caminada has produced architectural work in Surselva, Grisons that is unique in being directly determined by the ecological, geographical and structural engineering premises of the location and the lifestyles of its population.
The new edition includes the texts and project collection of Cul zuffel e l'aura dado and is extended to include a selection of more recent projects since 2015.
Edited by: Bettina Schlorhaufer.
Photos: Lucia Degonda
Articles by: Jürg Conzett, Peter Schmid, Peter Rieder, Walter Zschokke

296 Seiten, 22,5 × 29 cm
296 Abbildungen, 214 Skizzen/Pläne
Hardcover, fadengeheftet
CHF 138.– / EUR 126,–
deutsch/englisch
ISBN 978-3-03761-114-2

2nd edition of Cul zuffel e l'aura dado, extended to include new projects

296 pages, 22.5 × 29 cm
296 illustrations,
214 sketches/plans
Hardback, stitched
CHF 138.00 / EUR 126.00
German/English
ISBN 978-3-03761-114-2

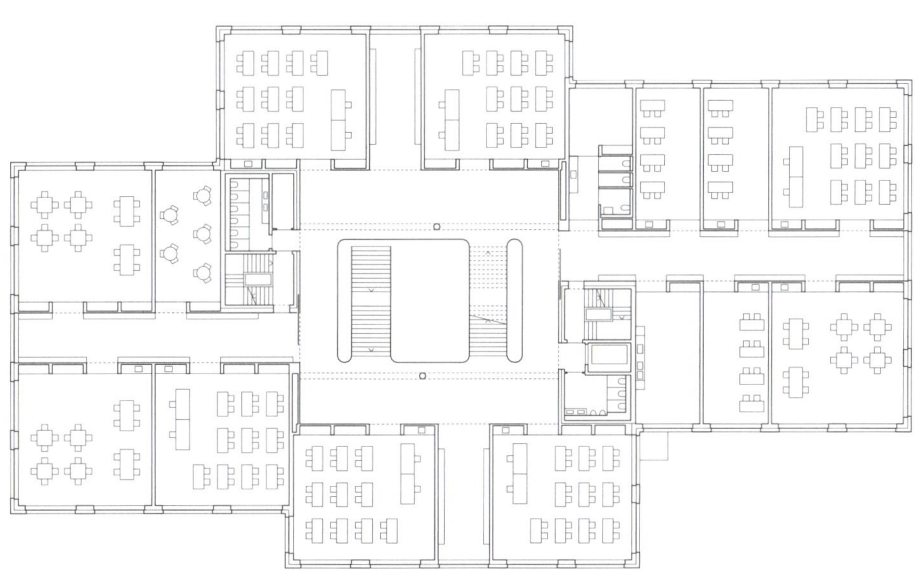

STADTENTWICKLUNG QUARTIER VIEUSSEUX-VILLARS-FRANCHISES, GENF

VIEUSSEUX-VILLARS-FRANCHISES URBAN EVOLUTION, GENEVA

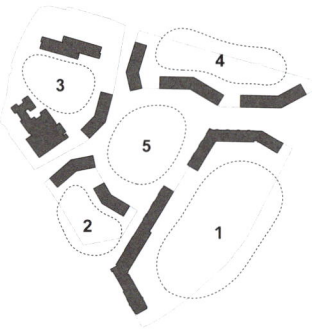

In seinem Streben nach Einheit greift der Entwurf zwei Charakteristika der gegenwärtigen städtischen Morphologie der Cité Vieusseux auf. Diese Morphologie resultiert aus der Entwicklung des vom Architekten Maurice Braillard nach dem Konzept des Mindestlebensraums konzipierten Quartiers aus den 1930er Jahren – der Entwurf verstärkt diese noch.

Auf der Südostseite definiert ein langer abgeknickter Baukörper eine Art vegetabile «Tasche», in der einzelne isolierte Gebäude Platz finden. Dieses Volumen zieht sich aus dem Quartierkern zurück und öffnet sich stattdessen nach aussen. Der Entwurf verfolgt dieses kontrastierende Prinzip, sodass die Bebauungsfläche in fünf Einzelräume unterteilt wird, die von Gebäuden begrenzt werden.

Diese Gliederung durch nach aussen geöffnete Ausbuchtungen wird direkt mit der Schaffung einer starken Zentralität assoziiert. Der Entwurf definiert das Herz des Quartiers neu und stärkt es in seiner Eigenschaft als Platz. Sechs Neubauten sind strassenseitig so angeordnet, dass sie friedvolle, mit hohen Bäumen bepflanzte Räume sowie im Zentrum einen grossen, offenen Hof mit Themengärten (Wassergarten, Spielgarten, Blumengarten, Gemüsegarten …) entstehen lassen. Die neuen Gebäude sind so platziert, dass eine direkte Frontalität vermieden wird. Sie bieten hochwertige optische Erweiterungen und definieren offene öffentliche Plätze, die untereinander verbunden sind.

Die erste Etappe der Quartiersverdichtung betrifft das Gebäude A, das sich in der kleinen Ausbuchtung im Südwesten befindet. Der Grundrisstyp setzt sich aus zwei Treppenhäusern zusammen, die 83 Wohnungen erschliessen. Je nach Standpunkt nimmt man den Baukörper als kleinen Riegel oder als ausgreifenden Block wahr.

In search of unity, this project takes up and reinforces two features of the current urban morphology of the Cité Vieusseux, a minimum-housing district designed by the architect Maurice Braillard that has developed since the 1930s.

Firstly, on the south-east side, a long existing folded volume creates a sort of vegetal "pocket" in which isolated constructions are placed. This volume folds back onto the district's interior and opens up the space towards its periphery. Based on this observation, the project proposes the pursuit of this principle; the site is thus broken down into five spaces that are lined by constructions.

Secondly, the arrangement of outward-looking pockets is directly associated with the creation of a strong centrality. The project redefines and reinforces the heart of the district as a square. On the street side, six new buildings form quiet spaces with high trees and, in the centre, a large open courtyard made up of themed gardens (water garden, playground, flower garden, vegetable garden…). The new buildings are structured in a way that avoids a direct frontage. They offer high-quality visual extensions and create open, interconnected public spaces.

The first neighbourhood-densification stage concerns building A, located in the small pocket to the south-west. The typical plan consists of two stairwells distributing 83 flats. Depending on the viewpoint, perception of the volume varies between a small bar and a radiant block.

Wettbewerb: 2013, 1. Preis
Realisierung: 2017–2021 (Bauabschnitt 1)
Bauherrschaft: SCHG
Wettbewerbsteam: Frédéric Bravard, Carlo Piffaretti, Marie-Laure Bourquin, Sven Hiestand
Projektteam: Delphine Ganter (Projektleitung und Bauleitung), Jessica Bertuzzi, Guy Detruche, Cecilia Lante, Alexandre Delencre, Alfredo Huertas
Tragwerk: edms SA
Fachplanung:
Hirt ingénieurs & associés SA (Heizung und Belüftung), srg-engineering (Sanitär), Tecnoconsult SA (Elektrik), Orqual SA (Brandschutz), AcouConsult Sàrl (Akustik)
Landschaftsarchitektur: Gilbert Henchoz architectes paysagistes associés SA

Competition: 2013, 1ˢᵗ Prize
Construction: 2017–2021 (Stage 1)
Client: SCHG
Competition team: Frédéric Bravard, Carlo Piffaretti, Marie-Laure Bourquin, Sven Hiestand
Project team: Delphine Ganter (Project and Construction Manager), Jessica Bertuzzi, Guy Detruche, Cecilia Lante, Alexandre Delencre, Alfredo Huertas
Civil engineer: edms SA
Specialist engineers: Hirt ingénieurs & associés SA (heating and ventilation), srg-engineering (S), Tecnoconsult SA (electrics), Orqual SA (fire safety), AcouConsult Sàrl (acoustics)
Landscape architecture: Gilbert Henchoz landscape architects associés SA

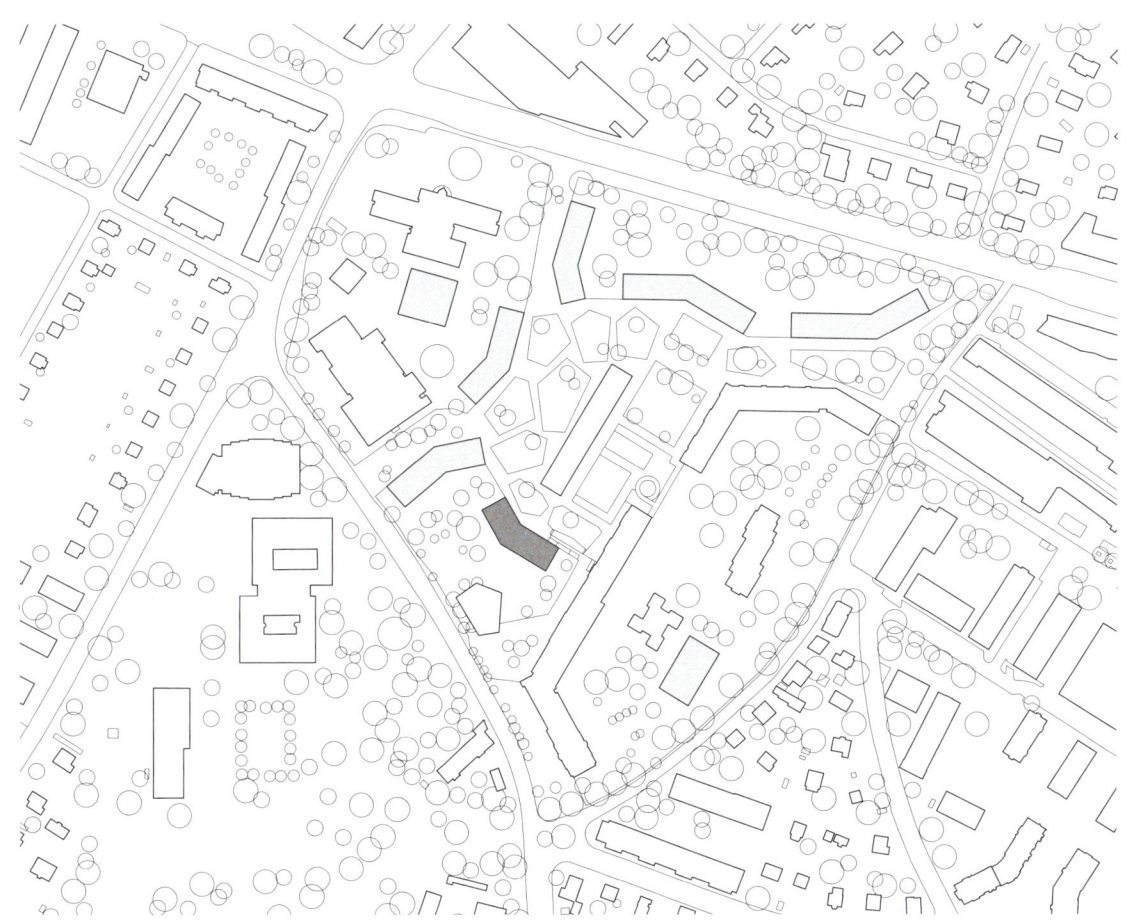

KINDERHEIM SERVAN, LAUSANNE

SERVAN CHILDREN'S HOME, LAUSANNE

Besondere Aufmerksamkeit galt der Integration des neuen Kinderheims in sein Umfeld. Das zwischen Bahnhof und See gelegene Quartier Sous-Gare zeichnet sich durch ein bemerkenswertes Stadtgefüge mit majestätischen Belle-Époque-Häusern, eleganten Strassen und mehreren Grünanlagen aus. Der gegliederte Baukörper weist Fassaden auf, die in Höhe und Breite denen der Nachbarhäuser ähneln. Dieser Wohnhauscharakter des unmittelbaren Umfelds wurde auch auf die Architektur des Heims angewandt, sodass ein behaglicher, sicherer Ort entstanden ist, der den Eindruck eines grossen, «den anderen gleichenden» Hauses vermittelt.

Die Küche nimmt eine zentrale Position im Hochparterre ein und steht in direkter Verbindung zum Haupteingang, den Treppenaufgängen und dem Fahrstuhl. Dies erleichtert die pädagogische Betreuung beim Zubereiten der Mahlzeiten und trägt dazu bei, eine intime häusliche Atmosphäre zu schaffen.

Bei den drei Wohneinheiten handelt es sich um Maisonettwohnungen, die über zwei Stockwerke gehen. In einem grossen Raum, der sich nach drei Seiten hin öffnet und durch eine Terrasse oder Loggia nach aussen eine Verlängerung erfährt, sind Wohn- und Esszimmer vereint. Alle Heimzimmer befinden sich in der zweiten Etage, wobei das Zimmer der Nachtwache eine zentrale Position einnimmt, damit diese ihrer Aufgabe leichter gerecht werden kann.

Die Dimensionen der Fenster und ihre materielle Umsetzung tragen zur Vereinheitlichung der verschiedenen Stiftungsbauten bei – Hort, Tageseinrichtung und neues Heim. Die Wahl von Rauputz für die Aussenfassaden hat sich logischerweise aufgedrängt, denn diese Art der Fassadenverkleidung ist im Wohnviertel vorherrschend und evoziert Domestizität.

Particular care was taken to integrate the new children's home into its context in the Sous-Gare district, between the station and the lake, which is characterised by a remarkable urban fabric formed by majestic Belle Époque houses, elegant avenues and several green spaces. Its volume is structured and generates façades of similar height and length to the neighbouring houses; their residential and domestic character is also used for the children's home to offer a comfortable and reassuring place, in the image of a large house that is "like the others".

The kitchen is centrally located on the upper ground floor, directly connected to the main entrance, stairs and lift. This arrangement facilitates educational care during the preparation of meals and helps create a domestic atmosphere.

Three living units are organised as maisonettes. A large combined living and dining room benefits from three aspects and external extensions – a terrace or loggia. All the bedrooms are grouped together on the second floor, with the caretaker's room in a central position to facilitate his job.

The window dimensions and the proposed markings contribute to unifying the different buildings of the foundation: a nursery, a day care centre and a new home. The choice of exterior plaster was logical; as the neighbourhood's dominant façade covering, it simply evokes domesticity.

Wettbewerb: 2014, 1. Preis
Realisierung: 2017–2019
Bauherrschaft: Fondation Bellet
Wettbewerbsteam: Frédéric Bravard, Valeriya Todorova
Projektteam: Juan Rodriguez (Projektleitung und Bauleitung), Alvise Allegretto, Valeriya Todorova, Jessica Bertuzzi, Alexandre Delencre, Carlo Piffaretti, Eliana Baretto
Tragwerk: Ingea SA
Fachplanung: Énergie Concept SA (Heizung, Belüftung und Sanitär), Betelec SA (Elektrik), Orqual SA (Brandschutz), BS Lucane Sàrl (Akustik)
Landschaftsarchitektur: MAP Monnier Architecture du Paysage SA

Construction: 2014, 1st Prize
Completion: 2017–2019
Client: Fondation Bellet
Competition team: Frédéric Bravard, Valeriya Todorova
Project team: Juan Rodriguez (Project and Construction Manager), Alvise Allegretto, Valeriya Todorova, Jessica Bertuzzi, Alexandre Delencre, Carlo Piffaretti, Eliana Baretto
Civil engineer: Ingea SA
Specialist engineers:
Énergie Concept SA (heating, ventilation and sanitary), Betelec SA (electrics), Orqual SA (fire safety), BS Lucane Sàrl (acoustics)
Landscape architecture: MAP Monnier Architecture du Paysage SA

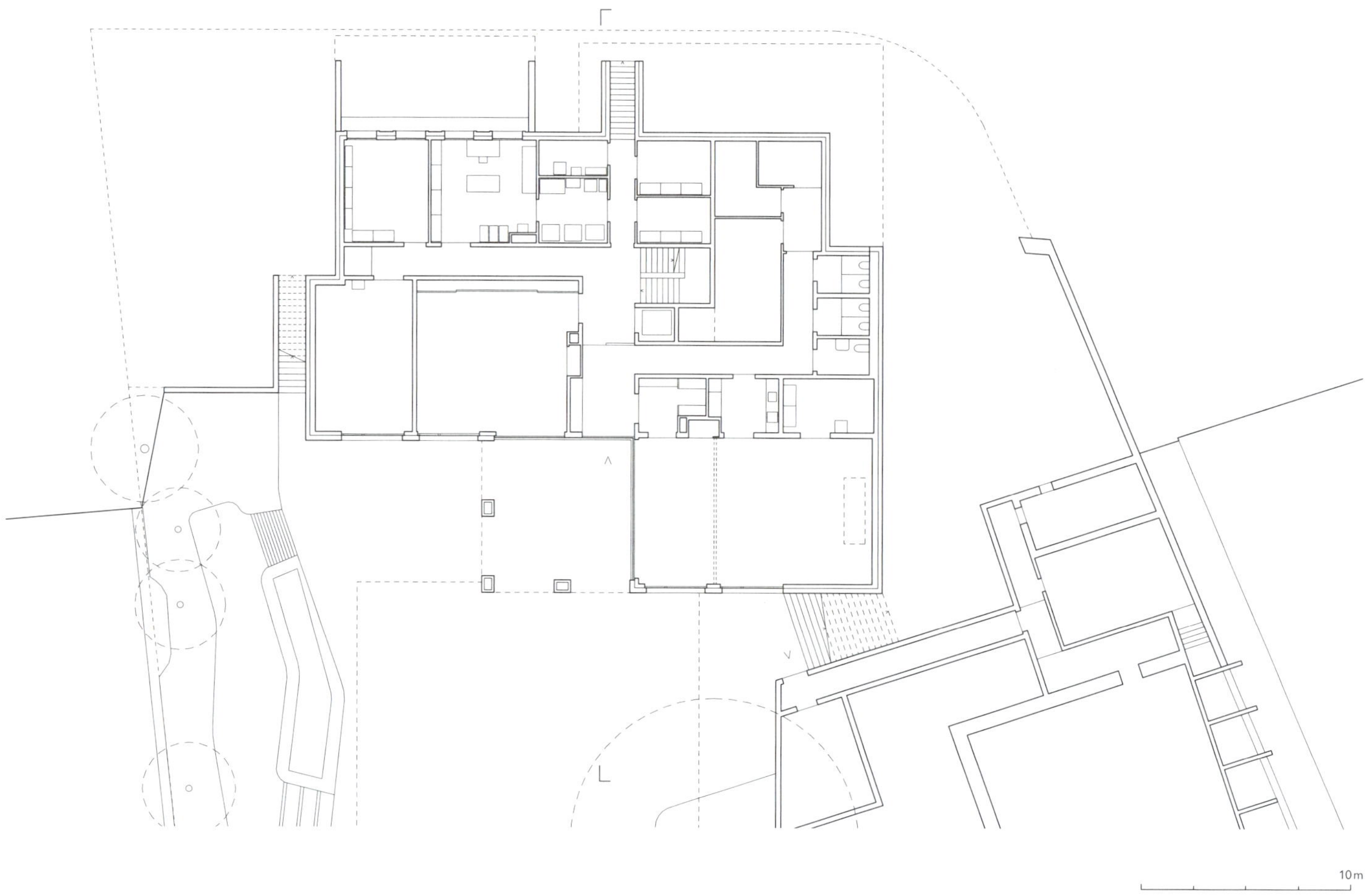

10 m

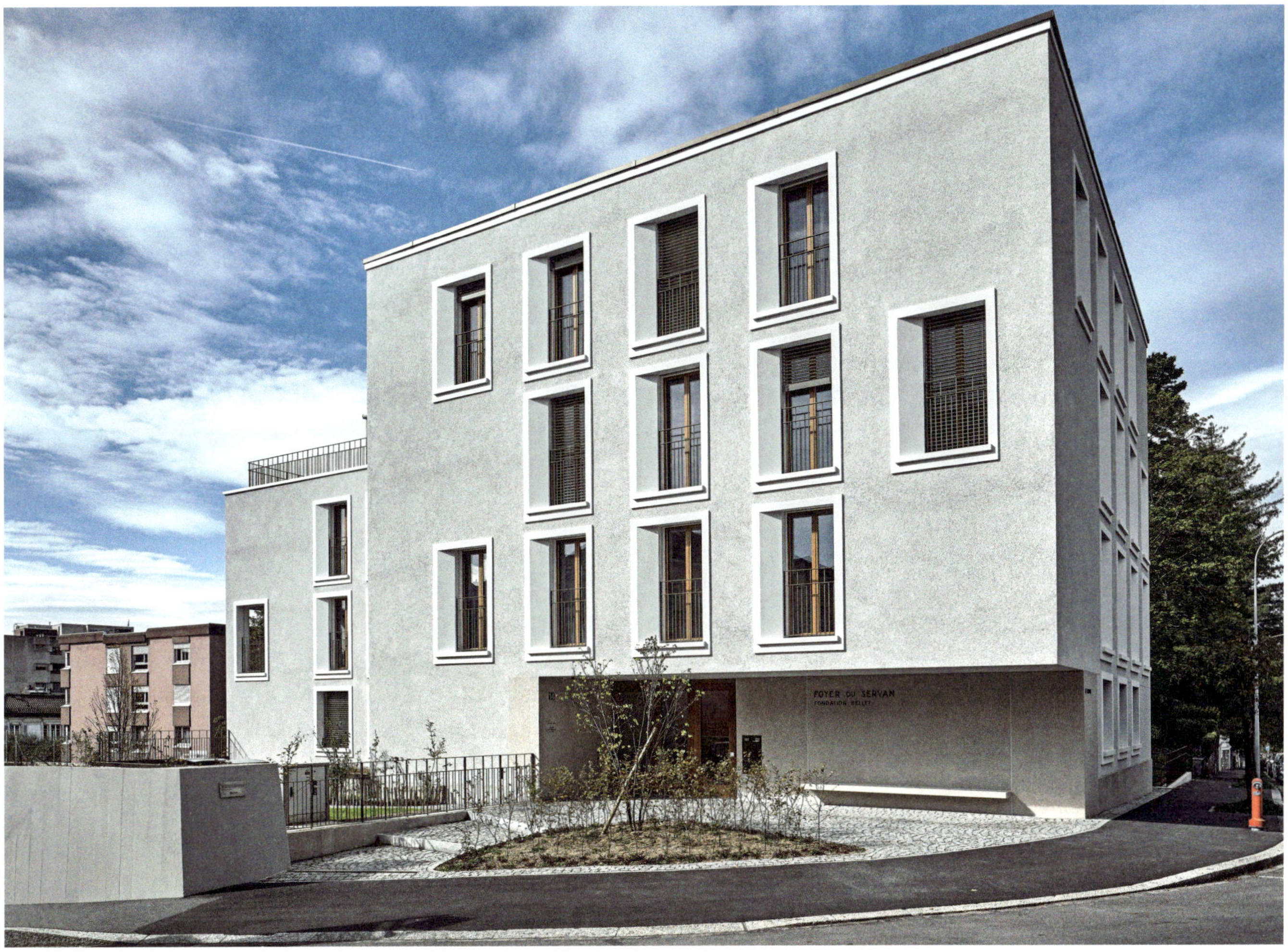
FOYER DU SERVAN
FONDATION BELLET

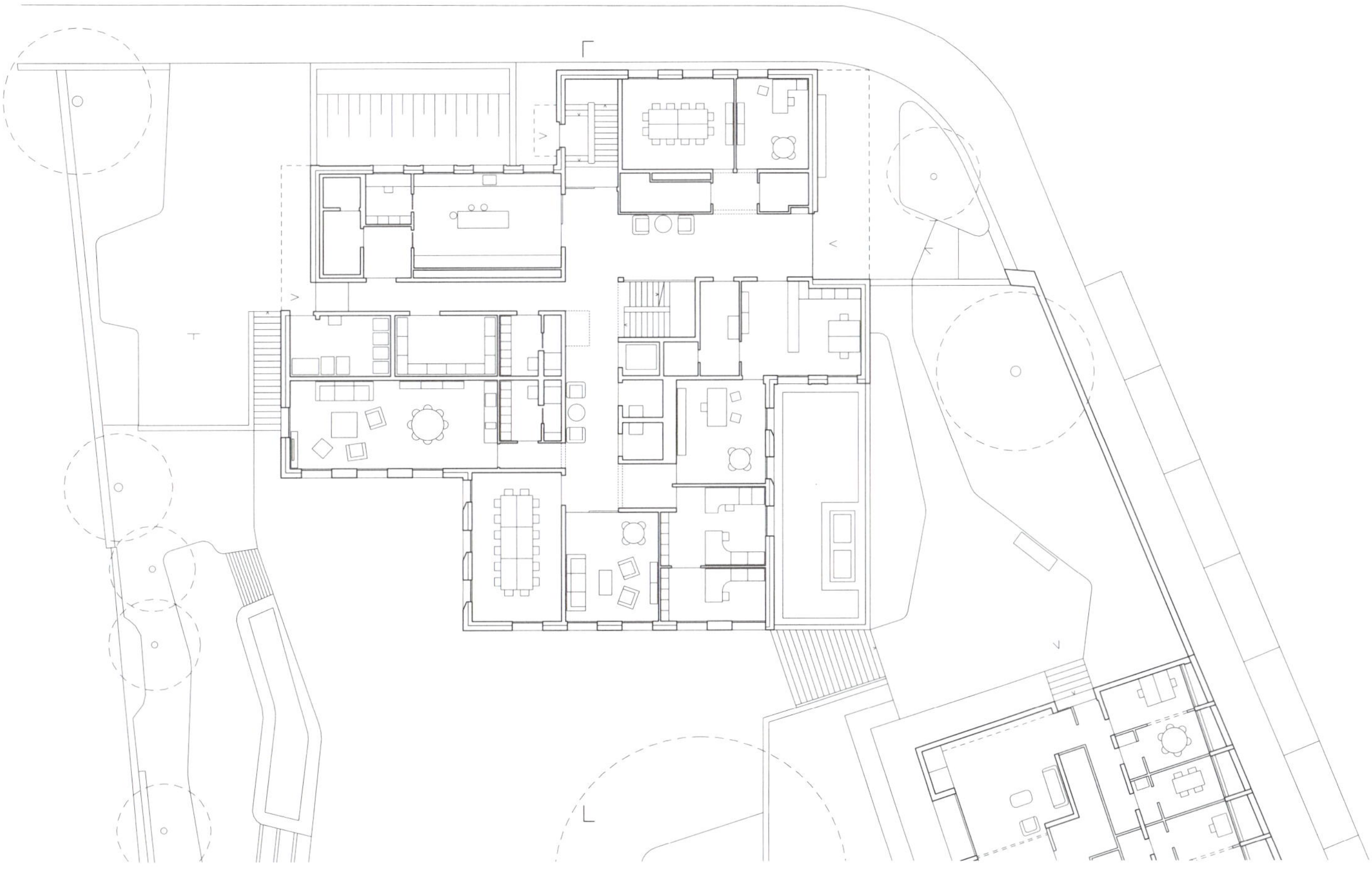

10 m

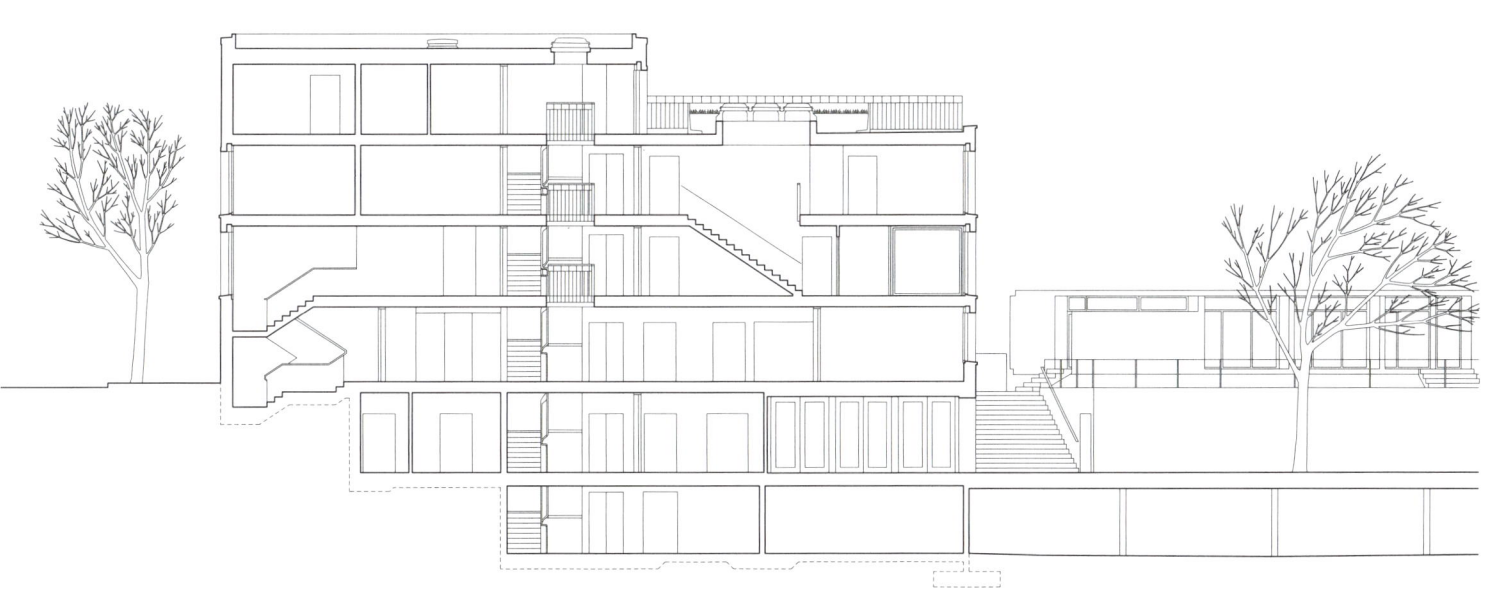

APARTMENTGEBÄUDE, CONFIGNON   RESIDENTIAL BUILDING, CONFIGNON

Das etwa 20 Minuten mit der Strassenbahn von Genf entfernte Confignon, das sich seinen dörflichen Charakter erhalten hat, wird durch den Bau neuer Wohnquartiere auf Gemeindegebiet innerhalb eines Jahrzehnts eine Einwohnerverdoppelung erfahren. Die im Norden des Ortes gelegene Parzelle, die durch zwei majestätische Zedern ihr besonderes Gepräge erhält, fordert geradezu die Ansiedlung eines neuen Wohngebäudes mit neun Apartments.

Das Gebäude, das die gleiche moderate Höhe aufweist wie die bereits existierenden Häuser, ist um die beiden Zedern herum konzipiert, sodass es diese «umspannt» und der künftigen Bewohnerschaft die Qualität bieten wird, inmitten einer baumbestandenen Grünanlage zu wohnen. Die Aussenanlagen wurden mehrheitlich unter Berücksichtigung der alten Bauten geplant, um die Auswirkungen auf das Wurzelsystem des Baumbestandes zu begrenzen und die versiegelten Flächen zu reduzieren.

Die Zedern wirken wie ein Eingangstor für die Wohnanlage an der Strassenecke. Ein Fussgängerweg von untergeordneter Landschaftswirkung führt zum Gebäude. Die Wegführung unter den Bäumen setzt sich in der Vertikalen über ein aussen liegendes Treppenhaus bis zur Dachterrasse fort.

Die gemeinsamen und zu den Baumkronen der Zedern hin geöffneten Treppenabsätze werden im Inneren der Wohnungen durch eine Abfolge von Räumen weitergeführt, die sich in der Diagonalen öffnen und den Eingang, das Esszimmer und das Wohnzimmer miteinander verbinden. Durch diese von der Mitte der Grünanlage und des Treppenhauses ausgehende strahlenförmige Anordnung können drei Wohnungen unterschiedlicher Grundfläche auf jeder Etage untergebracht werden: Das kleinste Apartment in der Mitte ist nach Westen hin ausgerichtet, während die grösseren Wohnungen an den beiden Enden ihr Sonnenlicht aus drei Richtungen beziehen.

Having preserved its village character, Confignon, some twenty minutes by tram from Geneva, will see its population double in a decade, following the construction of new districts on its territory. Located to the north of the village and characterised by the presence of two majestic cedar trees, the plot strongly constrains the location of a new building with nine apartments.

Maintaining a low profile similar to the existing houses, the building is structured around the two cedars to "embrace" them and offer the future inhabitants the benefits of living in the heart of a leafy park. Most of the exterior fittings are designed within the old buildings' right of way to limit the impact on their root system and reduce the impermeable surfaces.

The cedar trees evoke the entrance to the residence at the corner of the streets. A pedestrian path with minimal landscape impact leads to the building. The path under the trees develops vertically through an exterior stairwell to the rooftop terrace.

The common landings, open to the cedar treetops, are extended inside the dwellings by a succession of spaces that open diagonally and link the entrance, the kitchen-dining room and the living room. This radial progression from the heart of the park and the stairwell makes it possible to arrange three apartments of different sizes on each floor: the smallest, central apartment faces west, while the larger ones at the ends enjoy natural light from three sides.

Realisierung: 2019– (laufend)
Bauherrschaft: Privat
Team: Delphine Ganter (Projektleitung und Bauleitung), Ángel Lallana, Gabriela Pratas, Théo Richard, Caroline David
Tragwerk: edms SA
Fachplanung: Conti & Associés ingénieurs SA (Heizung, Belüftung und Sanitär), srg-engineering (Elektrik), AcouConsult Sàrl / BATJ SA (Akustik)
Landschaftsarchitektur: OA Paysage

Construction: 2019– (ongoing)
Client: Private
Team: Delphine Ganter (Project and Construction Manager), Ángel Lallana, Gabriela Pratas, Théo Richard, Caroline David
Civil engineer: edms SA
Specialist engineers: Conti & Associés ingénieurs SA (heating, ventilation and sanitary), srg-engineering (electrics), AcouConsult Sàrl / BATJ SA (acoustics)
Landscape architecture: OA Paysage

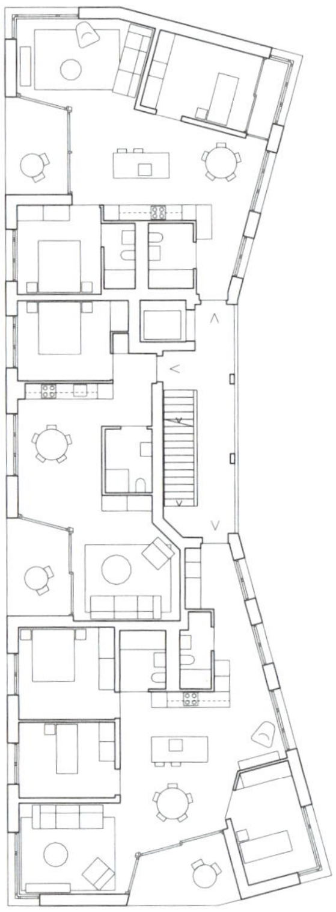

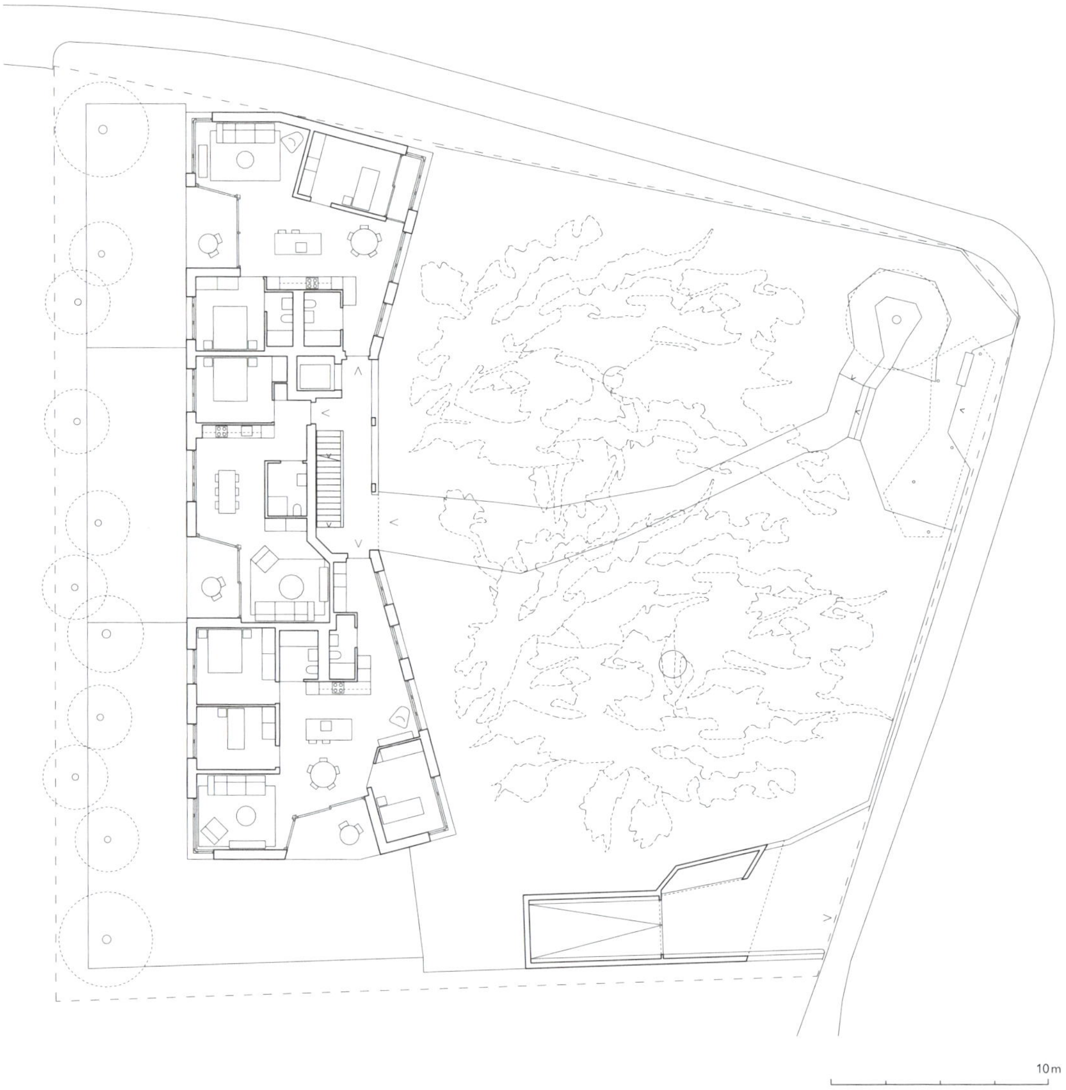

10 m

52

ÖFFENTLICHER RAUM AM BAHNHOF CORNAVIN, PLACE DE MONTBRILLANT, GENF

PUBLIC SPACES AT CORNAVIN MAIN STATION, PLACE DE MONTBRILLANT, GENEVA

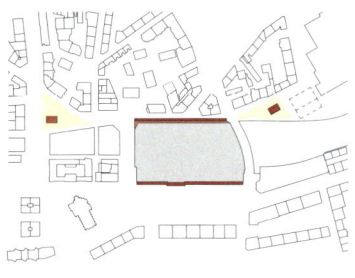

Auf der Suche nach einem zum Bild eines städtischen Bahnhofs passenden Massstabs, der jedoch den Wohncharakter des Quartiers Les Grottes nordwestlich des Hauptbahnhofs Cornavin berücksichtigt, wurde das Projekt in drei Sequenzen und Bauabschnitte unterteilt, die sich von der gleichen Architektursprache herleiten.

In der mittleren Sequenz wird die Place de Montbrillant auf der einen Seite durch eine neue Bahnhofsfassade bestimmt, welche die Proportionen des existierenden Gebäudes wiederaufnimmt; und auf der anderen Seite durch einen terrassenförmig angelegten Platz mit Baumbestand. Die Fassade und ihr Vordach zeichnen sich durch eine filigrane, z-förmig abgeknickte Struktur aus, die den Innenraum auf den Aussenraum projiziert. Das Konstruktionssystem aus einer Metallstruktur, die auf einem Minimum an Stützen auf dem Boden ruht, sowie einer Füllung mit Glastafeln verleiht dem Komplex einen leichten, lichten Charakter. Die sorgfältige Auswahl der Glasarten und deren Zusammensetzung lässt eine einzigartige Textur entstehen, welche an die Bahnhofsglasdächer des ausgehenden 19. Jahrhunderts, insbesondere an die des Bahnhofs Cornavin, erinnert.

Die seitlichen Sequenzen entsprechen den mit hohen Bäumen bepflanzten Plätzen, die eine Begrenzung des Raums durch die Vegetation bilden. Der Zugang zum Bahnhof erfolgt durch hell erleuchtete Häuschen, die in der Mitte dieser Plätze stehen.

Die vorgeschlagene Verdichtung des benachbarten Quartiers Les Grottes setzt auf eine Kontinuität der bestehenden städtischen Morphologie und ihrer spezifischen Besonderheiten. Die Strassenfront ist teilweise geschlossen, und zwei frei stehende Gebäude gegenüber den Eingängen sind zurückversetzt. Diese zurücktretenden Baukörper laden dazu ein, den Häuserblock zu durchqueren und erzeugen Raumkontinuitäten in Richtung des Parc des Cropettes.

In search of the right scale for the image of a main station, while respecting the domestic character of the Grottes district to the north-west of the main Cornavin station, the project is structured into three sequences and three interventions, stemming from the same architectural language.

In the central sequence, the Place de Montbrillant is defined on one side by a new station façade that reflects the proportions of the existing building and, on the other, by a stepped space planted with trees. The façade and its canopy are characterised by a filiform folded structure with a Z-shaped cross-section, which projects the interior space outwards. The construction system, consisting of a metal structure with a minimum of ground supports and clear glass tiles, gives the building a light and bright character. Careful work on the types of glass and assemblies generates a unique texture, evoking the glass roofs of late-19th-century stations, in particular those of Cornavin.

The two lateral sequences correspond to squares planted with high trees allowing the space to be delimited by vegetation. Access to the station is via illuminated kiosks located at the heart of these squares.

The densification proposal for the neighbouring Grottes block plays on the continuity with the existing urban morphology and its specifics. The street frontage is partially confirmed and two buildings are freely set back opposite the accesses. These recessed volumes invite people to cross the block and generate spatial continuities towards the Cropettes park.

Wettbewerb: 2020, 1. Preis
Realisierung: 2021– (laufend)
Bauherrschaft: Stadt Genf
Wettbewerbsteam: Gabriela Pratas
Projektteam: Gabriela Pratas (Projektleitung), Manuel Grosset
Tragwerk: edms SA
Fachplanung: Transitec (Mobilität), Lumière Électrique (Beleuchtung), Conti & Associés ingénieurs SA (Belüftung), Zanetti Ingénieurs-Conseils (Elektrik), srg-engineering (Brandschutz), BATJ SA (Akustik), BCS SA (Fassade)
Landschaftsarchitektur (Pilot): MAP Monnier Architecture du Paysage SA

Competition: 2020, 1st Prize
Construction: 2021– (ongoing)
Client: City of Geneva
Competition team: Gabriela Pratas
Project team: Gabriela Pratas (Project Manager), Manuel Grosset
Civil engineer: edms SA
Specialist engineers: Transitec (mobility), Lumière Électrique (lighting), Conti & Associés ingénieurs SA (ventilation), Zanetti Ingénieurs-Conseils (electrics), srg-engineering (fire safety), BATJ SA (acoustics), BCS SA (façade)
Landscape architecture (pilot): MAP Monnier Architecture du Paysage SA

KANTONSSCHULE CHABLAIS, AIGLE   CHABLAIS HIGH SCHOOL, AIGLE

Ziel des Projekts war, ein zweckmässiges und wirtschaftliches Konstruktionssystem aus Holz zu entwickeln, dieses als Prototyp bei der Kantonsschule Chablais inmitten eines stark im Wachstum begriffenen Ballungsgebietes am südöstlichen Ende des Genfersees anzuwenden und es dann mit Variationen für künftige nachobligatorische Bildungseinrichtungen des Kantons Waadt zu reproduzieren.

Sämtliche Funktionen sind in einem einzigen kompakten, in vier Teile untergliederten Baukörper von geringer Höhe zusammengefasst, der im Zentrum eines bewaldeten Parks liegt. Die Schule verfügt auf jeder der vier Seiten über einen Eingang, der jeweils in eine grosszügige Halle führt, um die herum strahlenförmig die wichtigsten öffentlichen Funktionen angeordnet sind.

Der Grundriss der beiden Etagen ist so angelegt, dass kurze, lichtdurchflutete Zugangsräume entstehen, die eine Verbindung zum Aussenraum aufweisen. Die Klassenräume, von denen sich ein Fernblick bietet, sind an der Gebäudeaussenseite angesiedelt, während die Funktionsräume im Zentrum um einen zentralen Innenhof sowie um zwei seitliche Innenhöfe herum gruppiert sind, die in den Pausen zugänglich sind.

Der leichte, transparente und lichtdurchlässige architektonische Charakter leitet sich direkt vom Konstruktionssystem ab. Das Holzgerüst ist innen wie aussen bewusst sichtbar belassen und trägt zu einer verstärkten Identifikation bei. Beim gesamten Bau wurde eine Rasterbreite von 275 Zentimetern eingehalten, was die Vorfertigung und den Transport erleichtert. Der Grundriss wurde entsprechend einer Klasseneinheit von jeweils 825 × 825 Zentimetern entworfen.

The project aims to develop a rational, innovative and economical wooden construction system and to apply it as a prototype to the Chablais high school within a growing agglomeration at the south-eastern end of Lake Geneva, and then to reproduce it with variations for future further educational establishments in the Canton of Vaud.

Located in the centre of a wooded park, the whole programme is gathered in a single compact volume, of low height, orientated and structured in four sections. The school has an entrance from each of the four directions, leading to a generous central hall around which the main collective functions radiate.

The plan of the two floors creates short, bright distribution spaces in contact with the outside. The classrooms are distributed around the periphery with views into the distance, while the special rooms are grouped in the centre around a large central patio and two side patios, accessible during the breaks.

The light, transparent and permeable architectural character is a direct result of the construction system. The wooden framework is deliberately kept visible both inside and outside, reinforcing identification with the building. The entire structure is built using a 275 cm wide grid, which facilitates prefabrication and transport. The plan is designed on the basis of an 825 × 825 cm class unit.

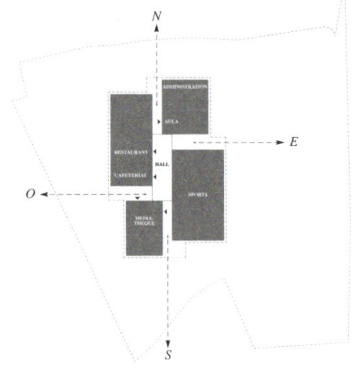

Wettbewerb: 2021, 1. Preis
Realisierung: 2021– (laufend)
Bauherrschaft: Kanton Waadt
Wettbewerbsteam: Gabriela Pratas, Alvise Allegretto, Alexandre Delencre, Guy Detruche, Théo Richard
Projektteam: Francesco Ricci (Projektleitung), Nicolas Choquard, Santiago Miguel, Egzon Goçi, João de Deus Ferreira, Théo Richard, Guy Detruche
Tragwerk: edms SA, Charpente Concept SA
Fachplanung: Weinmann-Énergies SA (Heizung, Belüftung, Sanitär und Umwelt), srg-engineering (Elektrik und Brandschutz), Gartenmann Engineering SA (Akustik)
Landschaftsarchitektur: Forster-Paysage Sàrl

Competition: 2021, 1ˢᵗ Prize
Construction: 2021– (ongoing)
Client: Canton of Vaud
Competition team: Gabriela Pratas, Alvise Allegretto, Alexandre Delencre, Guy Detruche, Théo Richard
Project team: Francesco Ricci (Project Manager), Nicolas Choquard, Santiago Miguel, Egzon Goçi, João de Deus Ferreira, Théo Richard, Guy Detruche
Civil engineers: edms SA, Charpente Concept SA
Specialist engineers: Weinmann-Énergies SA (heating, ventilation, sanitary and environment), srg-engineering (electrics and fire safety), Gartenmann Engineering SA (acoustics)
Landscape architecture: Forster-Paysage Sàrl

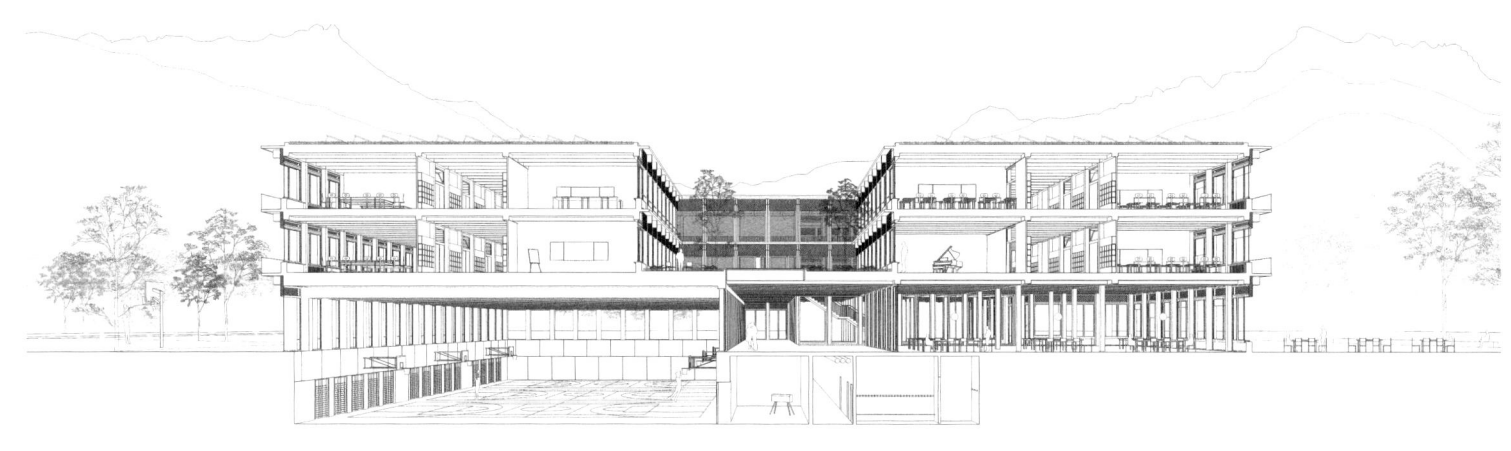

60

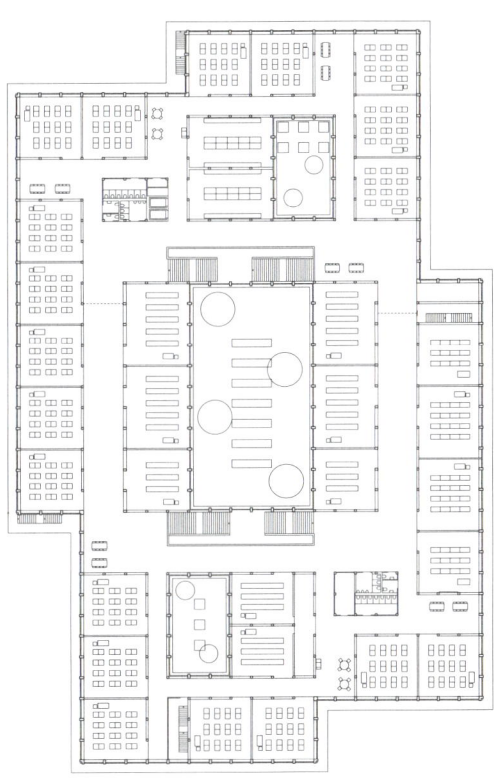

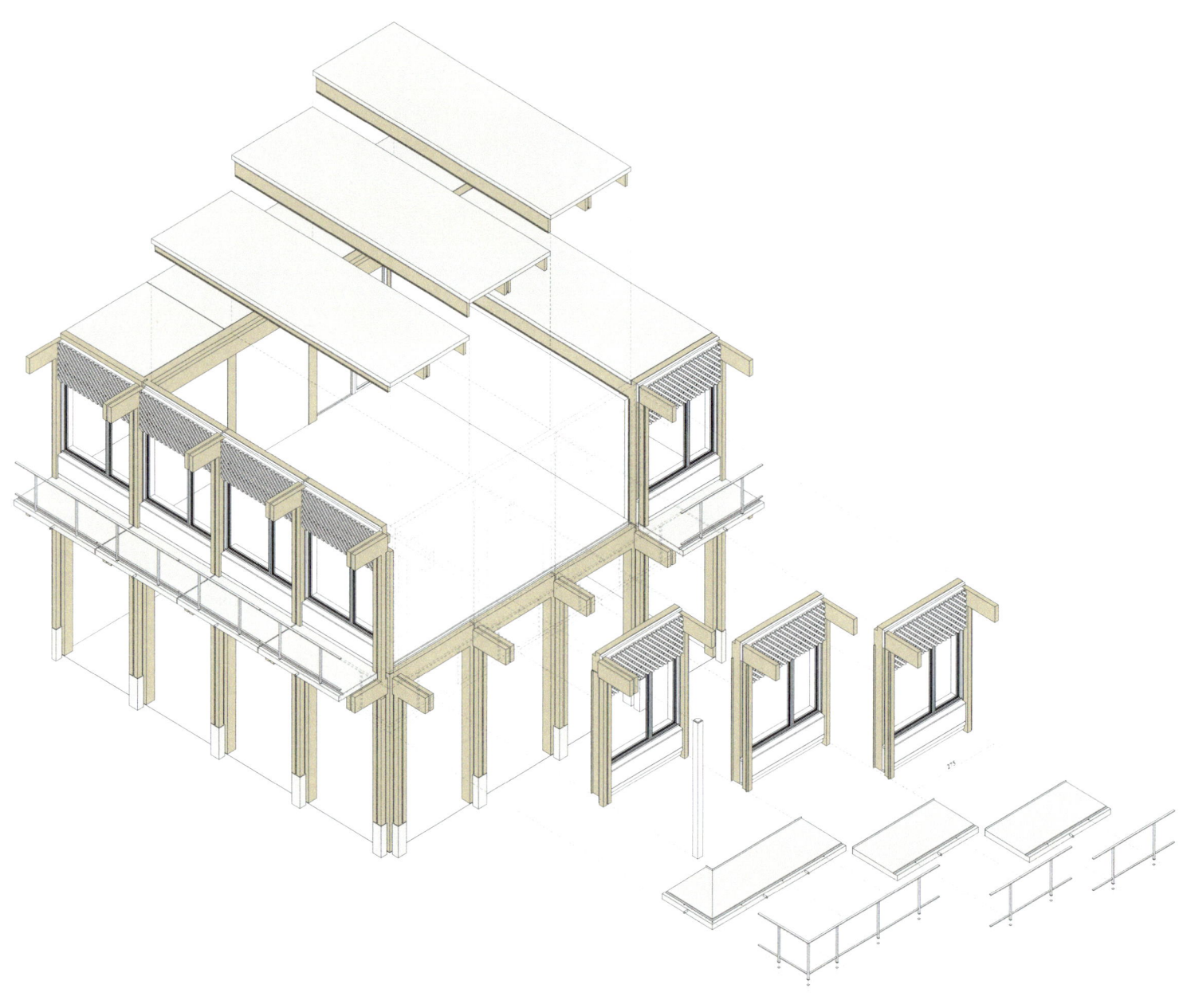

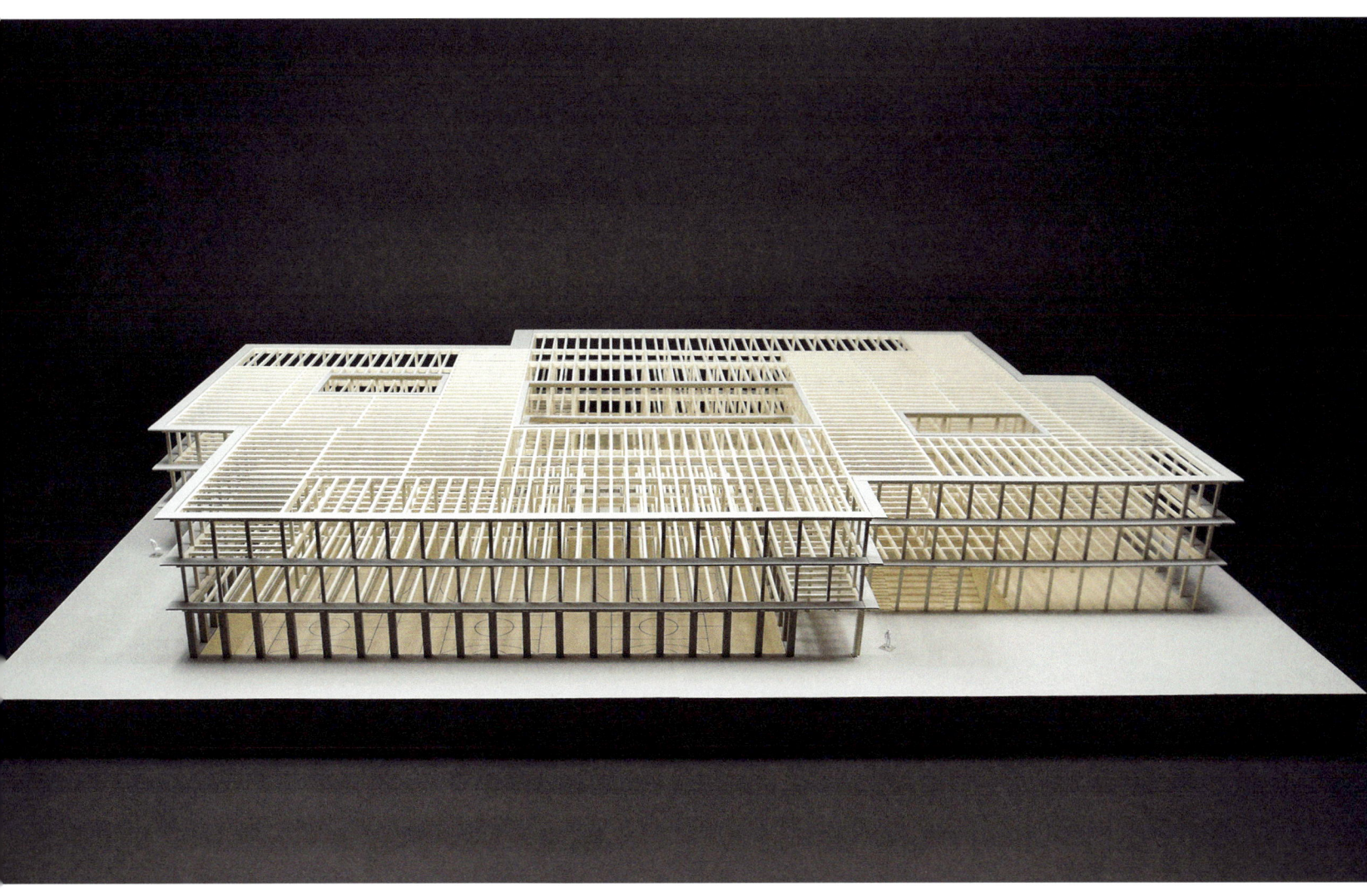

SCHULE BELVÉDÈRE, CHÊNE-BOUGERIES
BELVÉDÈRE SCHOOL, CHÊNE-BOUGERIES

50 Jahre nach dem Bau der Primarschule Belvédère unter der Leitung des Architekten Paul Waltenspühl am Stadtrand von Genf hat sich die Landschaft rund um das Schulhaus stark verändert und ist heute ein mit grossen Bäumen bepflanztes Areal. Das Projekt setzt die Schule und ihren Anbau im Herzen des Parks in Szene und stellt an allen Seiten durchlässige Verbindungen zu den angrenzenden Stadtteilen her. Ein Innenhof im Zentrum dient als neuer Mittelpunkt, der die Schule, den Anbau und den Park miteinander verbindet.

Die Klassenräume des Anbaus sind analog dem Altbau und entsprechend seiner Helixform in drei kleinere Bereiche unterteilt, die das Zusammengehörigkeitsgefühl und den Bildungsauftrag der Einrichtung unterstreichen. Alle Klassenzimmer sind nach zwei Seiten hin ausgerichtet, grosszügig mit Licht durchflutet und bieten unterschiedliche Perspektiven auf die sie umgebende Natur.

Das bestehende Gebäude bleibt im Hinblick auf den Denkmalschutz vollständig erhalten und wird durch die Tatsache aufgewertet, dass der Anbau mit seinem komplementären architektonischen Charakter in das Landschaftsbild eingebettet ist.

Fifty years after the Belvédère primary school was built by the architect Paul Waltenspühl on the outskirts of Geneva, the setting has greatly developed and nowadays it is a planted area featuring large trees. The project sets the school and its extension in the middle of the park and creates permeable connections with the neighbouring districts on all sides. The design of a central courtyard provides a new place of reference linking the school, its extension and the park.

Just like the existing school, and drawing on its helical shape, the classrooms of the extension are grouped in small units of three, marking a sub-scale that promotes a sense of belonging and the educational mission of the establishment. All classrooms are dual-aspect, providing generous natural light and several visual openings to the surrounding vegetation.

From a heritage point of view, the existing building is fully preserved and enhanced by the background presence of the extension, its complementary character merging into the landscape.

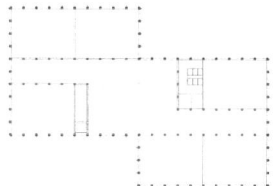

Grundrissschema der spiralförmigen Erweiterung mit drei Klassenzimmern in kleinen Einheiten gruppiert
Floor plan diagram of the helical shape extension with three classrooms grouped in small units

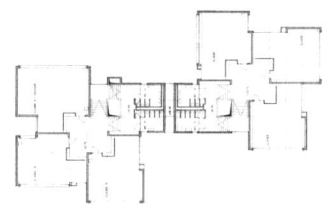

Schule Belvédère, Bauabschnitt 2 der Erweiterung, 1972.
Architekt: Paul Walthenspühl
**Belvédère School, construction phase 2 of extension project, 1972.
Architect: Paul Walthenspühl**

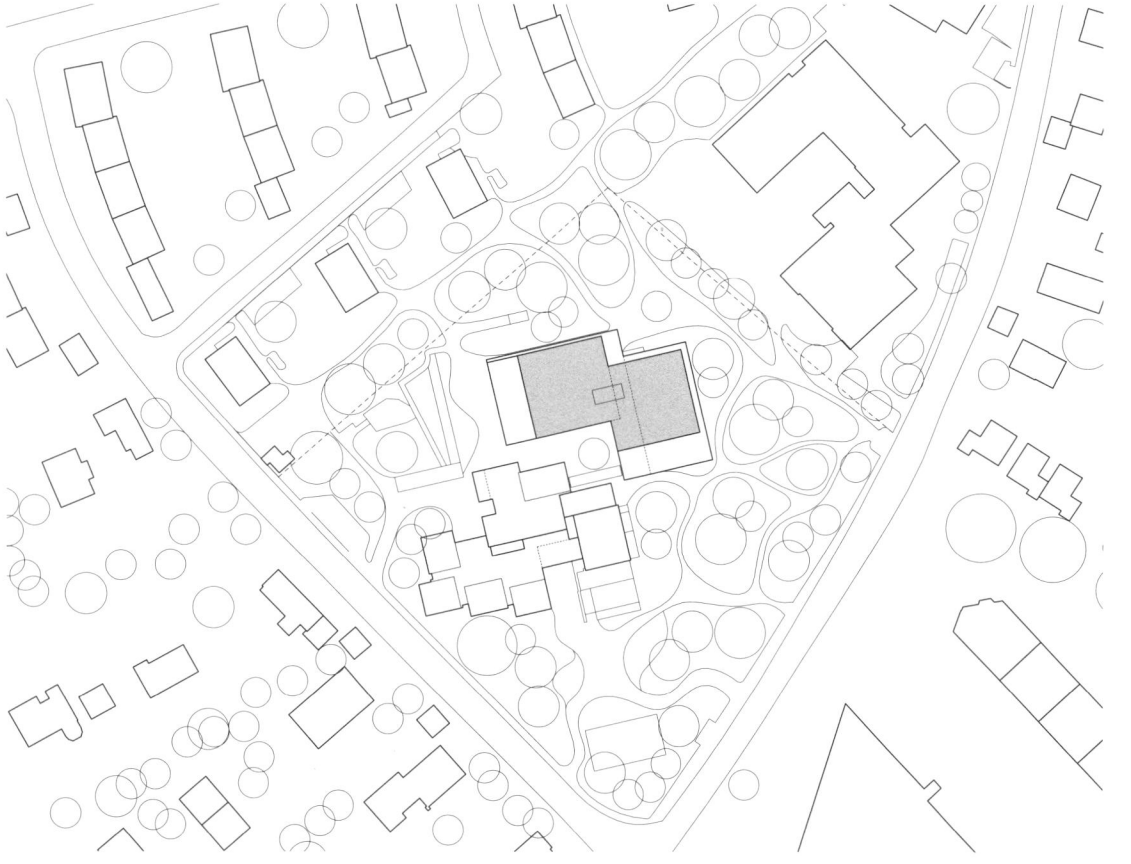

Wettbewerb: 2022, 1. Preis
Realisierung: 2022– (laufend)
Bauherrschaft:
Gemeinde Chêne-Bougeries
Wettbewerbsteam: Gabriela Pratas, Francesco Ricci, Nicolas Choquard, Téo Hubmann, Caroline David
Projektteam: Frédéric Bravard, (Projektleitung), Caroline David, Alexandre Gameiro, João D. Ferreira
Tragwerk: edms SA
Fachplanung: Conti & Associés ingénieurs SA (Heizung und Belüftung), Ryser Eco Sàrl (Sanitär), DSSA SA (Elektrik), srg-engineering (Brandschutz), Architecture & Acoustique (Akustik)
Landschaftsarchitektur: apaar Sàrl

**Competition: 2022, 1st Prize
Construction: 2022– (ongoing)
Client:
Municipality of Chêne-Bougeries
Competition team: Gabriela Pratas, Francesco Ricci, Nicolas Choquard, Téo Hubmann, Caroline David
Project team: Frédéric Bravard (Project Manager), Caroline David, Alexandre Gameiro, João D. Ferreira
Civil engineer: edms SA
Specialist engineers:
Conti & Associés ingénieurs SA (heating and ventilation),
Ryser Eco Sàrl (sanitary), DSSA SA (electrics), srg-engineering (fire safety), Architecture & Acoustique (acoustics)
Landscape architecture: apaar Sàrl**

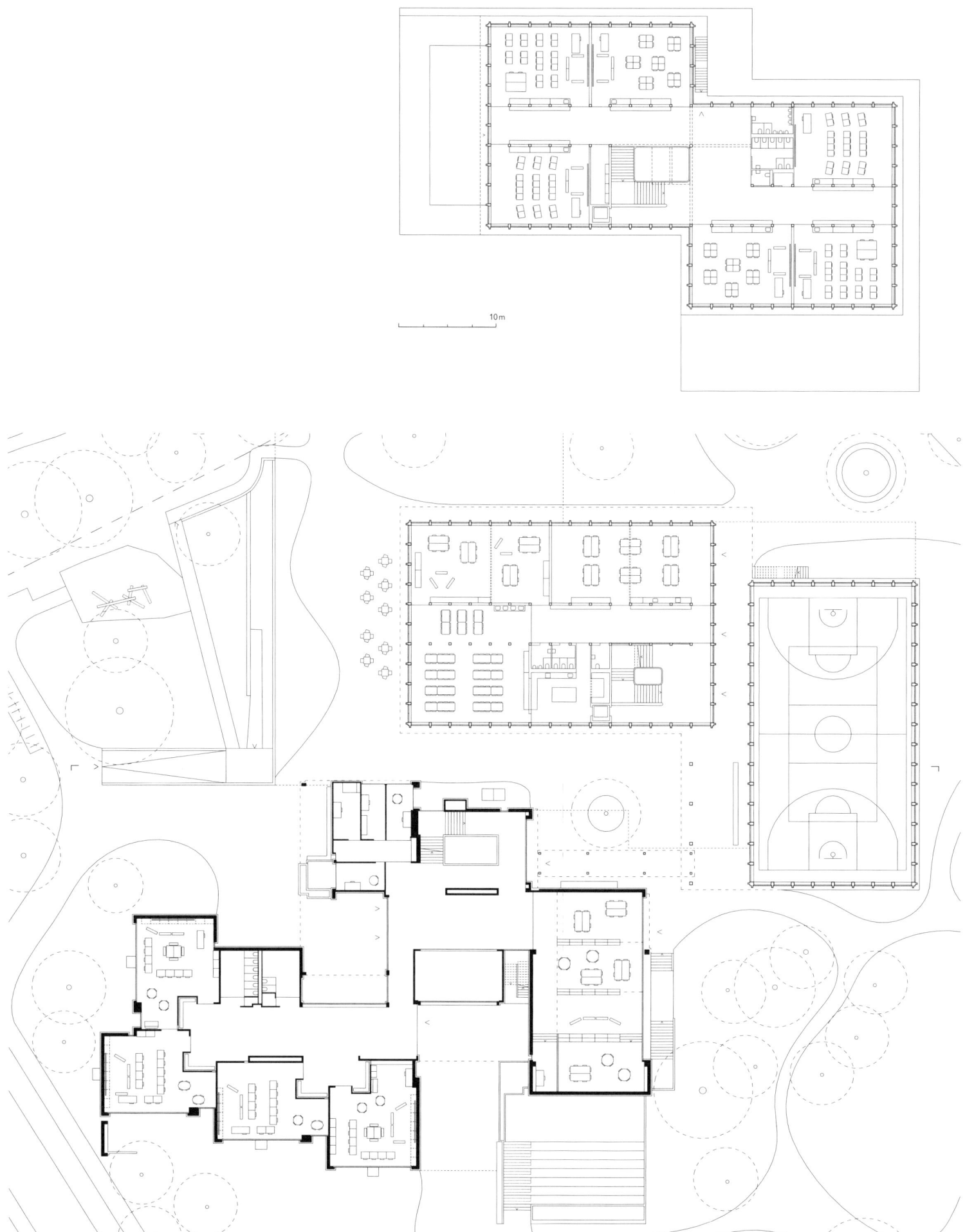

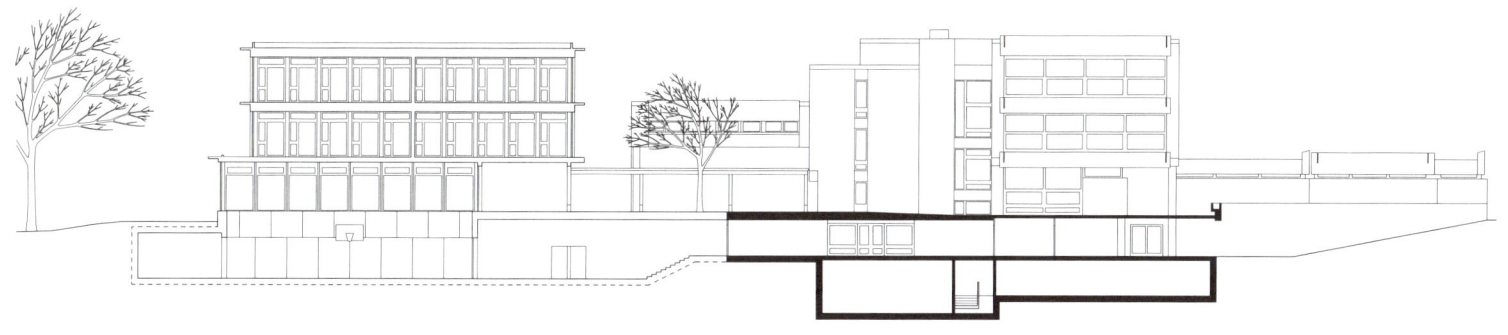

HOCHSCHULE FÜR GESUNDHEIT, GENF
SCHOOL OF HEALTH SCIENCES, GENEVA

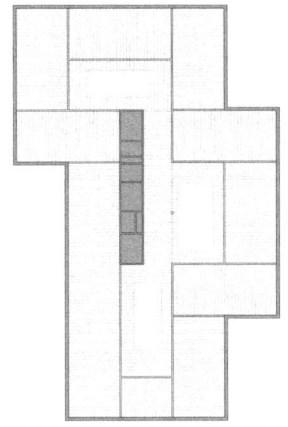

Die Parzelle liegt in Nähe der Genfer Universitätskliniken auf der grünen Westseite des Plateau de Champel. Der Ort zeichnet sich durch seine sanfte Hanglage mit einer sehr grossen Pflanzendichte und -vielfalt aus. Die Hauptintention des Entwurfs besteht ganz offensichtlich darin, die landschaftlichen Elemente des Geländes zu wahren und zur Geltung zu bringen. Die gegliederte Form des Baukörpers, die sich von der Organisation des Gebäudes ableitet, erlaubt die Aufteilung der Fassaden in mehrere Facetten, sodass keine lange Gebäudefront entsteht, sondern der Eindruck eines Volumens, das sich gut in sein Umfeld einfügt. Die drei unterschiedlichen Gebäudezugänge befinden sich auf drei verschiedenen Seiten, wodurch das gesamte Gelände rund um die Hochschule eine Funktion erhält.

Die Innenraumaufteilung ist in drei übereinanderliegende funktionale Einheiten gegliedert, nämlich in die für Publikum zugänglichen Räumlichkeiten, die Unterrichtsräume und die Forschungsabteilung. Die Gesamtheit der Räume verteilt sich auf drei Etagen rund um drei Höfe, die den Grundriss und die Verteilung im Gebäude organisieren: Die Räume sind jeweils strahlenförmig um einen solchen Raum herum angeordnet. Diese Höfe, die von oben Licht ins Herz des Baukörpers einfallen lassen, sind jeweils mit einer Treppe ausgestattet, die eine fliessende, schnelle Wegführung gewährleistet und damit den Studierenden wie dem Lehrkörper die Orientierung erleichtert.

Das Konstruktionssystem trägt dazu bei, den Bedarf an grauer Energie zu begrenzen. Tragende Fassaden aus Stahlbetonfertigteilen wurden mit Holz- und Betonverbunddecken kombiniert.

Close to the Geneva University Hospitals, the plot is located on the green western slope of the Champel plateau. The spirit of the place is characterised by a very high density and diversity of vegetation on a gently sloping hillside. The primary intention of the project is clearly to maintain and enhance the landscape elements of the site. The structured form of the volume, resulting from the organisation of the building, allows the façades to be split into several facets, not generating a long building front and enhancing the perception of a template that is well integrated into the context. Each of the three differentiated entrances is located on a different side, allocating functions to the whole site around the school.

The interior organisation is structured in three superimposed functional entities, namely those that are accessible to the public, the teaching rooms, and the research offices. All the rooms are spread over three levels around three courtyards that organise the layout and distribution space: they "unfold" in a ring around this space. Allowing zenithal light to penetrate to the heart of the volume, the courtyards each have a staircase that generates fluid and rapid routes, thereby helping students and teachers to get around.

The construction system contributes to limiting the need for embodied energy. Load-bearing façades made of prefabricated, reinforced concrete elements are combined with structural floor slabs made of wood and concrete.

Wettbewerb: 2018, 2. Preis
Bauherrschaft: Kanton Genf
Wettbewerbsteam: Alvise Allegretto, Alexandre Delencre, Egzon Goçi, Théo Richard
Tragwerk: edms SA
Landschaftsarchitektur: MAP Monnier Architecture du Paysage Sàrl

Competition: 2018, 2ⁿᵈ Prize
Client: Canton of Geneva
Competition team: Alvise Allegretto, Alexandre Delencre, Egzon Goçi, Théo Richard
Civil engineer: edms SA
Landscape architecture: MAP Monnier Architecture du Paysage Sàrl

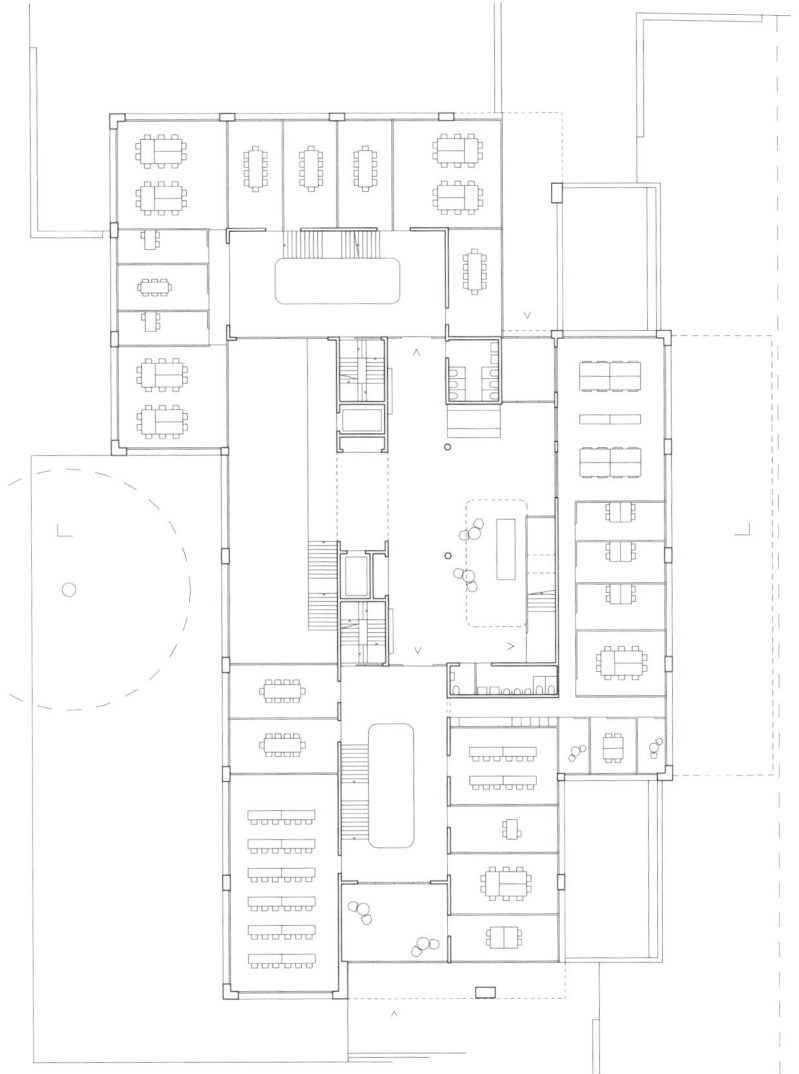

10 m

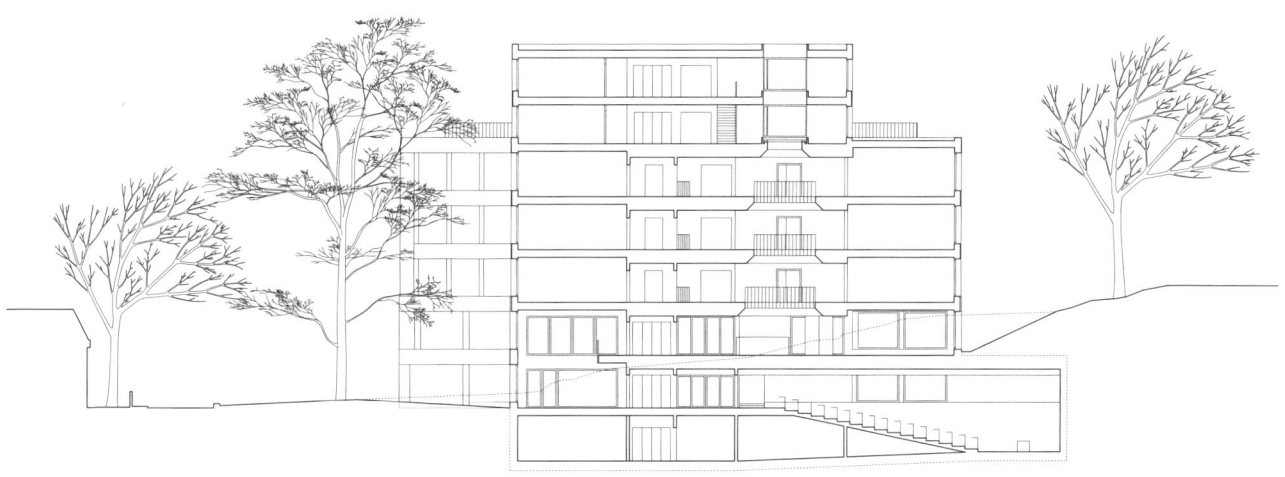

SCHULZENTRUM ES II, MEYRIN
ESII SCHOOL GROUP, MEYRIN

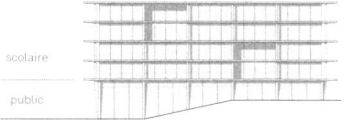

Das für diesen wichtigen Komplex aus Sekundarschule und Sportanlage vorgeschlagene Gelände in unmittelbarer Nachbarschaft zu Meyrin Cité – der ersten «Satellitenstadt» in der Schweiz, in den 1960er Jahren nordwestlich von Genf hinter dem Flughafen konzipiert – profitiert von seiner Randlage, die angesichts der ländlichen Umgebung auf Nachhaltigkeit ausgelegt ist.

Ausgehend von der Idee, einen Park zu definieren und soviel wie möglich von dem Baumbestand zu erhalten, kombiniert der Entwurf Sporthalle und Unterrichtszimmer innerhalb eines gegliederten Baukörpers auf verschiedenen Ebenen und lässt eine maximale Bodenfläche frei. Für die Anlage der Dreifachsporthalle wurde die 6 Meter tiefer gelegene Senke einer alten Kiesgrube genutzt. Durch den gegliederten Grundriss und die Freiflächen im Erdgeschoss konnten die Teilräume des Parks miteinander verbunden und in alle Himmelsrichtungen führende Wege angelegt werden.

Die Schule verfügt über zwei getrennte Eingänge, die durch Aussparungen in den an die Dreifachsporthalle angrenzenden Teilen definiert sind. Zwei lichtdurchflutete Atrien führen in den ersten Stock, wo über der Sporthalle die Wegführung und Verteilung erfolgt. Die vier Obergeschosse sind durch vier offene Treppen miteinander verbunden, die sich um Höfe und Atrien verteilen. Der Grundriss wird durch eine ringförmige Anordnung der Klassenzimmer bestimmt, die so in verschiedene Richtungen orientiert sind.

Das Projekt ist als Passivbau konzipiert, dessen Architektur auf eine natürliche Belüftung der Innenräume setzt. Das hybride Konstruktionssystem, bei dem Holz, Beton und Lehm kombiniert sind, bietet eine optimale Antwort auf aktuelle Bau- und Umweltfragen. Die Tektonik sowie die Proportionen und die filigrane Gliederung der Fassaden bestimmen den luftigen, strahlenden Charakter eines Gebäudes, das behutsam in einen Park integriert wurde.

Directly beside Meyrin Cité, the first "satellite city" in Switzerland, which was designed in the 1960s to the north-west of Geneva after the airport opened, the proposed site for this important secondary education and sports complex benefits from a peripheral location that is destined to remain, facing the agricultural landscape.

Starting from the idea of developing a park and preserving as much as possible of the existing grove, the project superimposes the sports and school programmes within a single, structured volume, freeing up a maximum amount of open space. The layout of the triple sports hall draws on the depression of a former gravel pit located six metres below. The structured layout, together with the open spaces on the ground floor, allows the sub-spaces of the park to be linked, offering routes in all directions.

The school has two distinct entrances defined by recesses in the areas adjacent to the triple hall. Two bright atriums lead to the first floor, where the circulation above the volume occupied by the triple sports hall takes place. The four upper levels are connected by four open staircases arranged around courtyards and atriums. The plan is defined by a ring of classrooms around the perimeter, offering different orientations.

The project is conceived as a passive building with architecture that allows natural interior ventilation. Combining wood, concrete and raw earth, the hybrid construction system offers an ideal response to current construction and environmental issues. The tectonics, as well as the proportions and the façades' filiform design, define the airy, radiant character of a building that is delicately set in the park.

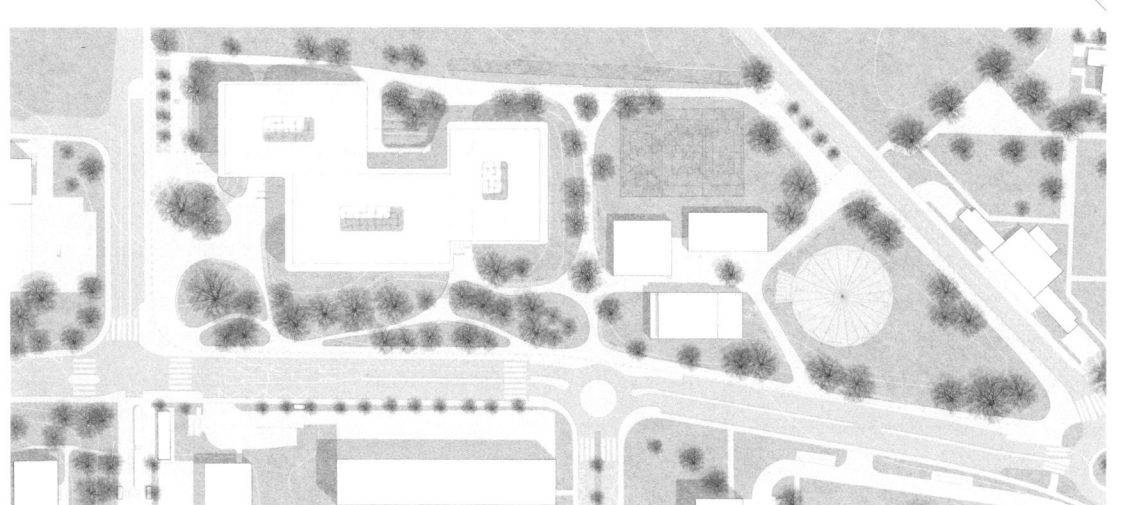

Wettbewerb: 2019, 3. Preis
Bauherrschaft: Kanton Genf
Wettbewerbsteam: Alvise Allegretto, Alexandre Delencre, Egzon Goçi, Guy Detruche
Tragwerk: edms SA
Fachplanung: Estia SA (Thermik)
Landschaftsarchitektur: MAP Monnier Architecture du Paysage Sàrl

Competition: 2019, 3rd Prize
Client: Canton of Geneva
Competition team: Alvise Allegretto, Alexandre Delencre, Egzon Goçi, Guy Detruche
Civil engineer: edms SA
Thermal engineer: Estia SA
Landscape architecture: MAP Monnier Architecture du Paysage Sàrl

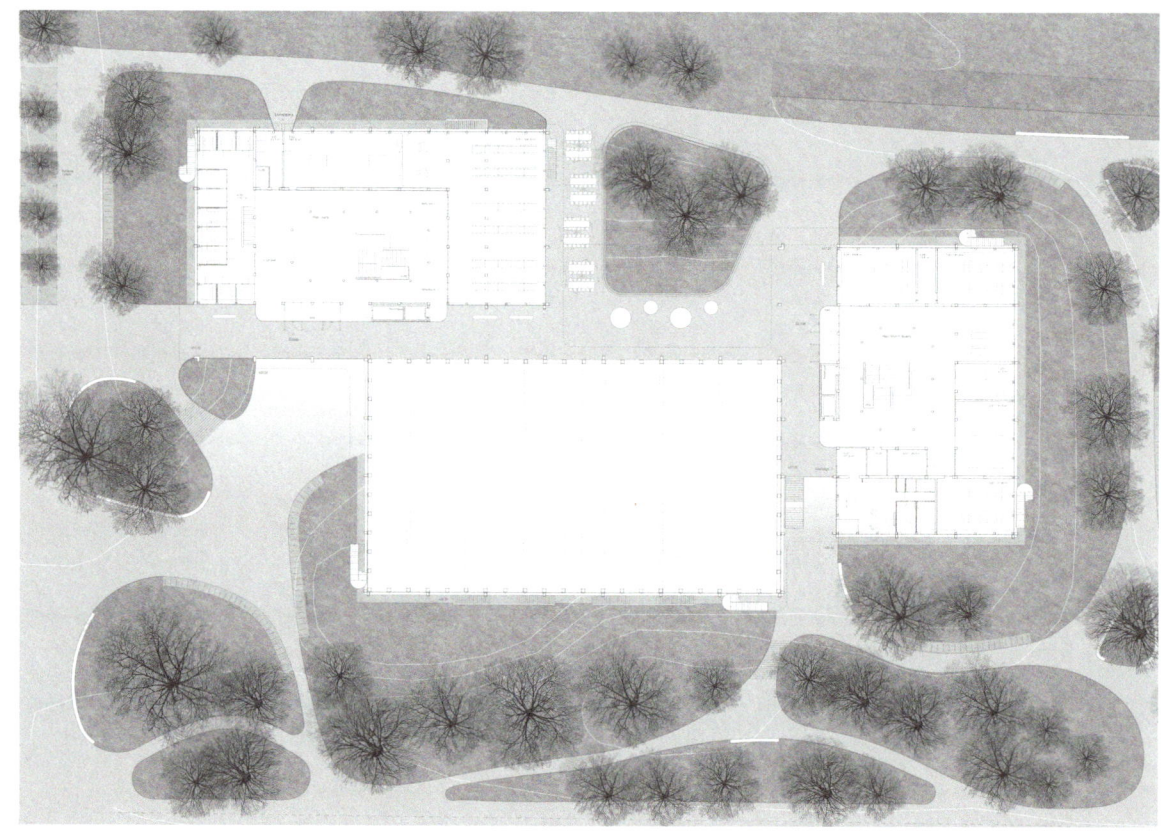

74

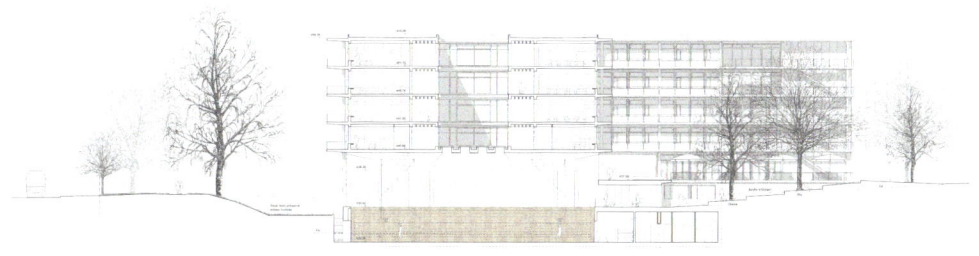

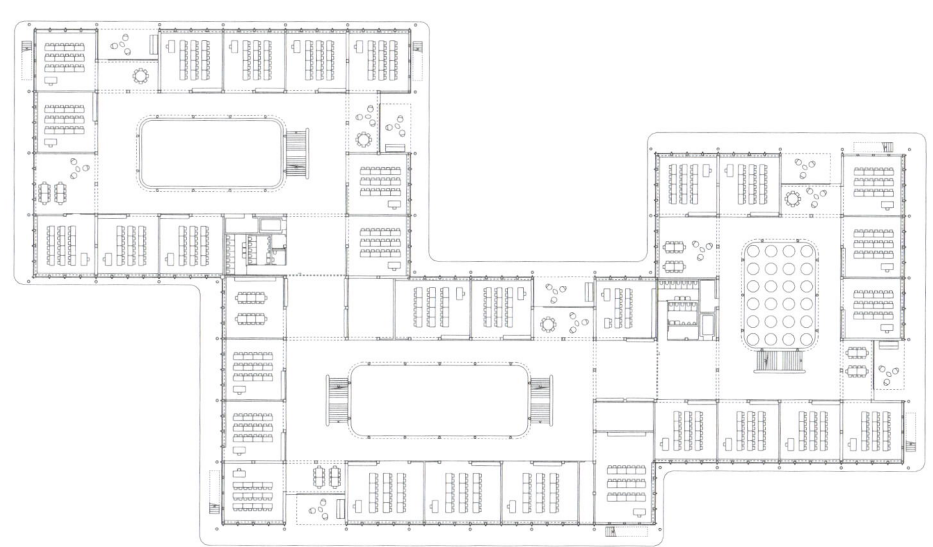

WERKVERZEICHNIS
Auswahl Bauten, Projekte und Wettbewerbe

2005		Entwurf Hauserweiterung, Renens
2006		Entwurf Wohnüberbauung, Vernier
		Wettbewerb Sporthalle und Grundschule, Châtel-Saint-Denis
2007		Umbau Wohnhaus, Veyrier
		Wettbewerb Sporthalle und Schulanlage, Attalens (5. Preis)
		Wettbewerb Müllverwertungsanlage und Räumlichkeiten der Müllabfuhr, Saint-Prex
		Umbau eines alten Bauernhauses in Familienbesitz, Landecy (mit Isabelle Irlé-Martin)
		Entwurf Hausumbau, Vessy
2008		Umbau Apartment, Carouge
		Wettbewerb Kommunales Mehrgenerationenhaus, Saint-Cergue (mit Darius Golchan; 1. Preis)
2009		Wettbewerb Erweiterung Kinderkrippe Le Gazouillis, Genf (5. Preis)
		Umbau Wohnhaus, Plan-les-Ouates
		Umbau Wohnhaus, Collonge-Bellerive
		Wettbewerb Apartmentgebäude Les Communailles, Onex (mit Darius Golchan; Auswahlverfahren)
		Umbau Apartment, Eaux-Vives, Genf
		Wettbewerb Kommunales Mehrzweckgebäude, Pregny-Chambésy (mit Bonhôte Zapata)
2010		Haus in den Bergen, Leysin
		Wettbewerb Anlage mit Schule und öffentlichen Einrichtungen, Parc des Cropettes, Genf
		Entwurf Apartmentgebäude, Pully
2011		Umbau Wohnhaus, Vésenaz
		Wettbewerb Apartmentgebäude Petite-Boissière, Genf
		Wettbewerb Schweizer Pavillon auf der Expo 2015 in Mailand
		Umbau Wohnhaus, Thônex
2012	1	Wettbewerb Apartmentgebäude im Chemin Dr J.-L. Prévost, Genf (3. Preis)
		Wettbewerb Schulanlage Triangle des Pervenches, Carouge
		Umbau Arztpraxis, Champel
2015	2	Wettbewerb Apartmentgebäude Les Saules, Genf (Auswahlverfahren)
		Kinderheim Uttins, Yverdon-les-Bains
		Umbau Wohnhaus, Chêne-Bougeries
2016		Umbau Einzimmerwohnung, Paris
		Umbau Kinderheim, Lausanne
	3	Wettbewerb Unternehmensgebäude der EMS Les Tines, Nyon (4. Preis)
	4	Privathaus, Grimisuat
		Wettbewerb Campus Santé, Lausanne
		Umbau Wohnung in Champel, Genf
	5	Entwurf Wohnüberbauung, Chêne-Bougeries
2017		Wettbewerb Neue Orientierungsschule Le Renard in Balexert, Genf
	6	Wettbewerb Schule Belvédère, Lausanne
2018		Wettbewerb Hochschule für Gesundheit [Haute École de Santé], Genf (2. Preis)
		Erweiterung Komplex mit Schule und Rathaus (Bauabschnitt 1), Satigny (Wettbewerb 2010, 1. Preis)
2019	7	Wettbewerb École des Vernets, Genf (4. Preis)
	8	Wettbewerb Provisorischer Sitzungssaal für die Vereinten Nationen, Genf (Preisträger)
		Kinderheim Servan, Lausanne (Wettbewerb 2014, 1. Preis)
		Umbau Kinderheim, Renens (Entwurf, noch nicht abgeschlossen)
2020	9	Wettbewerb Heim und Kinderhort Sainte Famille, Renens (4. Preis)
		Wettbewerb Schulzentrum ESII, Meyrin (3. Preis)
2021		Stadtentwicklung Quartier Vieusseux-Villars-Franchises, Genf (Wettbewerb 2013, 1. Preis)
	10	Wettbewerb Erweiterung Schulkomplex, Corsier (4. Preis)
2022		Erweiterung Komplex mit Schule und Rathaus (Bauabschnitt 2), Satigny (Wettbewerb 2010, 1. Preis)

Laufende Projekte:
Erweiterung Komplex mit Schule und Rathaus (Bauabschnitt 3), Satigny (Wettbewerb 2010, 1. Preis)
Apartmentgebäude, Confignon (Entwurf 2018)
Öffentlicher Raum am Bahnhof Cornavin, Place de Montbrillant, Genf (Wettbewerb 2020, 1. Preis)
Kantonsschule Chablais, Aigle (Wettbewerb 2021, 1. Preis)
Umbau Wohnhaus, Anières (Entwurf 2021)
Erweiterung Schule Belvédère, Chêne-Bougeries (Wettbewerb 2022, 1. Preis)

1

2

3

4

5

6

7

8

9

10

LIST OF WORKS
Selection of buildings, projects and competitions

2005		Study, house extension project, Renens
2006		Study, clustered housing project, Vernier
		Competition, sports hall and primary school, Châtel-Saint-Denis
2007		Conversion, house, Veyrier
		Competition, sports hall and school equipment, Attalens (5th Prize)
		Competition, waste disposal and road service premises, Saint-Prex
		Conversion, heritage farm, Landecy (with Isabelle Irlé-Martin)
		House conversion project, Vessy
2008		Apartment conversion, Carouge
		Competition, communal intergenerational building, Saint-Cergue (with Darius Golchan; 1st Prize, not built)
2009		Competition, extension Crèche Le Gazouillis, Geneva (5th Prize)
		House conversion, Plan-les-Ouates
		House conversion, Collonge-Bellerive
		Competition, Les Communailles residential building, Onex (with Darius Golchan; selection procedure)
		Apartment conversion, Eaux-Vives, Geneva
		Competition, multi-purpose municipal building, Pregny-Chambésy (with Bonhôte Zapata)
2010		Mountain house, Leysin
		Competition, school and public facilities, Parc des Cropettes, Geneva
		Project study, residential building, Pully
2011		House conversion, Vésenaz
		Competition, residential building Petite-Boissière, Geneva
		Competition, Suisse Expo Pavillon 2015 Milano
		House conversion, Thônex
2012	1	Competition, residential building, Chemin Dr J.-L. Prévost, Geneva (3rd Prize)
		Competition, school equipment, Triangle des Pervenches, Carouge
		Conversion, medical practice, Champel
2015	2	Competition, Les Saules residential building, Geneva (selection procedure)
		Uttins children's home, Yverdon-les-Bains
		House conversion, Chêne-Bougeries
2016		Studio conversion, Paris
		Conversion, children's home, Lausanne
	3	Competition, EMS Les Tines, Nyon (4th Prize)
	4	Detached house, Grimisuat
		Competition, Health Campus, Lausanne
		Apartment conversion, Champel, Geneva
	5	Clustered housing, Chêne-Bougeries (project, not built)
2017		Competition, new Orientation Cycle from Renard to Balexert, Geneva
	6	Competition, Belvédère School, Lausanne
2018		Competition, School of Health Sciences, Geneva, (2nd Prize)
		Stage 1 – School and Town Hall complex extension, Satigny (competition 2010, 1st Prize)
2019	7	Competition, Vernets School, Geneva (4th Prize)
	8	Temporary conference room, UN Geneva (award-winning project, not built)
		Servan children's home, Lausanne (competition 2014, 1st Prize)
		Conversion, children's home, Renens (project, pending)
2020	9	Competition, Sainte Famille home and daycare, Renens (4th Prize)
		Competition, ESII school group, Meyrin (3rd Prize)
2021		Vieusseux-Villars-Franchises Urban Evolution, Geneva (competition 2013, 1st Prize)
	10	Competition school group extension, Corsier (4th Prize)
2022		Stage 2 – School and Town Hall complex extension, Satigny (competition 2010, 1st Prize)

Ongoing projects:
Stage 3 – School and Town Hall complex extension, Satigny (competition 2010, 1st Prize)
Residential building, Confignon (project 2018)
Public spaces at Cornavin Main Station,
Place de Montbrillant, Geneva (competition 2020, 1st Prize)
Chablais High School, Aigle (competition 2021, 1st Prize)
House conversion, Anières (project 2021)
Extension, Belvédère School, Chêne-Bougeries (competition 2022, 1st Prize)

TIMOTHÉE GIORGIS

1974	Geboren in Lausanne
1994–2000	Diplom an der École Polytechnique Fédérale de Lausanne (EPFL) bei Professor Martin Steinmann
1997	Praktikum bei Philippe Gueissaz, Sainte-Croix, Waadt
1998	Praktikum bei Bischoff & Azzola Architekten, Zürich
2001	Praktikum bei Atelier In Situ, Montreal
2001–2006	Projektleiter bei Aeby & Perneger, Genf
2006	Gründung des Büros Timothée Giorgis architecte EPFL
2006–2010	Assistent von Professor Luca Ortelli, EPFL
2009	Mitglied des Schweizerischen Ingenieur- und Architektenvereins (SIA), Sektion Genf
2012	Gründung des Büros Timothée Giorgis Architectes Sàrl
2013–2017	Privatdozent HES-SO für Architekturplanung und Konstruktion, HEPIA Genf
2019	Gründung des Büros Giorgis Rodriguez Architectes Sàrl
2020–	Mitglied des Bundes Schweizer Architektinnen und Architekten (BSA), Sektion Genf

JUAN RODRIGUEZ

1976	Geboren in Biel
1994–2000	Diplom an der École Polytechnique Fédérale de Lausanne (EPFL) bei Professor Martin Steinmann
1997	Praktikum bei Marc Ryf Architekten, Zürich
2000–2002	Architekt bei Marc Ryf Architekten, Zürich
2002–2006	Projektleiter, dann Architekt und Teilhaber bei Alison Brooks Architects, London
2006–2014	Projektleiter bei Empty, Madrid
2015–2019	Projektleiter, dann Architekt und Teilhaber bei Timothée Giorgis Architectes, Genf
2015–	Mitglied des Schweizerischen Ingenieur- und Architektenvereins (SIA), Sektion Genf
2019	Gründung des Büros Giorgis Rodriguez Architectes Sàrl

MITARBEITENDE

Alvise Allegretto, Frédéric Bravard, Martial Buisson, Nicolas Choquard, Caroline David, Estelle Delavy, João De Deus Ferreira, Kristel Gabella (Verwaltung), Alexandre Gameiro, Delphine Ganter, Egzon Goçi, Sven Grams, Manuel Grosset (Praktikant), Ángel Lallana, Santiago Miguel, Gabriela Pratas, Francesco Ricci, Théo Richard, Chiara Sorrentino (Auszubildende)

EHEMALIGE MITARBEITENDE

Eliana Barreto, Jessica Bertuzzi, Jonas Bornand, Marie-Laure Bourquin, Florian Bouvier, Marion Cruz, Alexandre Delencre, Guy Detruche, Ricardo Do Rego, Miguel Fernandes, Sven Hiestand, Téo Hubmann, Alfredo Huertas, Cindy Lachat, Cecilia Lante, Miruna Maldarescu, Lyes Mekroud, Kevin Navarro, Carlo Piffaretti, Andrea Riva, Santino Schepisi, Denis Sermaxhaj, Valeriya Todorova, Giacomo Giorgio Zwygart

VORTRÄGE

2013	«Concours Vieusseux-Villars-Franchises – dialogues/exposition», HEPIA Genf, 15. Mai

BIBLIOGRAFIE

2008	Nicole Beetschen, «Séduisant projet pour réunir jeunes et vieux» [Kommunales Mehrgenerationenhaus, Saint-Cergue], in: *La Côte*, 8. September, S. 7
2011	«Bois découverte» [Haus in den Bergen, Leysin], in: *Les visites Lignum*, S. 12
2013	«Vieusseux gagne 600 logements» [Stadtentwicklung Quartier Vieusseux-Villars-Franchises, Genf], in: *Tribune de Genève*, 9. März
	«Un nouvel espace de vie» [Stadtentwicklung Quartier Vieusseux-Villars-Franchises, Genf], in: *Bâtir*, April, S. 8
	«Le nouveau souffle d'une coopérative» [Stadtentwicklung Quartier Vieusseux-Villars-Franchises, Genf], in: *Le Temps*, 3. April, S. 19
	Vincent Borcard, «Les ailes du désir» [Stadtentwicklung Quartier Vieusseux-Villars-Franchises, Genf], in: *Habitation*, Nr. 2, S. 4–9
	Mary-Luce Boand Colombini, «De la chenillle au papillon» [Stadtentwicklung Quartier Vieusseux-Villars-Franchises, Genf], in: *Efficience 21*, Nr. 7, S. 8
	«Des architectes genevois remportent un concours international» [Stadtentwicklung Quartier Vieusseux-Villars-Franchises, Genf], in: *Domotech*, Nr. 3, S. 6–11
	«Aménagement des places publiques à Genève» [Stadtentwicklung Quartier Vieusseux-Villars-Franchises, Genf], in: *Interface*, Nr. 18, S. 26–27
	Vincent Borcard, «Zusammenarbeit will gelernt sein» [Stadtentwicklung Quartier Vieusseux-Villars-Franchises, Genf], in: *Wohnen*, Nr. 11, S. 32–34
	[Haus in den Bergen, Leysin], in: *CHALETS. Trendsetting Mountain Treasures*, Salenstein, S. 202–205
2016	«Le Servan fête ses 100 ans et construit pour l'avenir» [Kinderheim Servan, Lausanne], in: *24 heures*, 23. Februar
2019	«Groupe scolaire des Vernets, Genève – Espaces multiusages» [Schulzentrum Les Vernets, Genf], in: *hochparterre.wettbewerbe*, Februar, S. 44–45
	Cahiers suisses des concours d'architecture, Nr. 2, Mai
	[Gemeinde- und Ratssaal, Satigny], in: Schweizerischer Ingenieur- und Architektenverein (SIA), Sektion Waadt (Hrsg.), *À voir, architectures romandes 2017–2019*, S. 132
2020	Christian Bernet, «La Ville aménage le futur espace entre Cornavin et le quartier des Grottes» [Öffentlicher Raum am Bahnhof Cornavin, Place de Montbrillant, Genf], in: *Tribune de Genève*, 18. Dezember, S. 7
	Gustavo Kuhn, «Le nord de la gare en plus vert et piéton» [Öffentlicher Raum am Bahnhof Cornavin, Place de Montbrillant, Genf], in: *Le Courrier*, 18. Dezember, S. 5

TIMOTHÉE GIORGIS

1974	Born in Lausanne
1994–2000	École Polytechnique Fédérale de Lausanne (EPFL) diploma under Professor Martin Steinmann
1997	Internship at Philippe Gueissaz, Sainte-Croix VD
1998	Internship at Bischoff & Azzola Architekten, Zurich
2001	Internship at Atelier In Situ, Montréal
2001–2006	Project Manager at Aeby & Perneger, Geneva
2006	Founded Timothée Giorgis architect EPFL
2006–2010	Assistant to Professor Luca Ortelli, EPFL
2009	Member, SIA Geneva section
2012	Founded Timothée Giorgis Architectes Sàrl
2013–2017	Lecturer, HES-SO Architecture and Construction Project, HEPIA Geneva
2019	Founded Giorgis Rodriguez Architectes Sàrl
2020–	Member, Federation of Swiss Architects (FSA), Geneva section

JUAN RODRIGUEZ

1976	Born in Bienne
1994–2000	École Polytechnique Fédérale de Lausanne (EPFL) diploma under Professor Martin Steinmann
1997	Internship at Marc Ryf Architekten, Zurich
2000–2002	Architect at Marc Ryf Architekten, Zurich
2002–2006	Project Manager, then Associate Architect at Alison Brooks Architects, London
2006–2014	Project Manager at Empty, Madrid
2015–2019	Project Manager, then Associate Architect at Timothée Giorgis Architectes, Geneva
2015–	Member, Swiss Society of Engineers and Architects (SIA), Geneva section
2019	Founded Giorgis Rodriguez Architectes Sàrl

COLLABORATORS

Alvise Allegretto, Frédéric Bravard, Martial Buisson, Nicolas Choquard, Caroline David, Estelle Delavy, João De Deus Ferreira, Kristel Gabella (administration), Alexandre Gameiro, Delphine Ganter, Egzon Goçi, Sven Grams, Manuel Grosset (intern), Ángel Lallana, Santiago Miguel, Gabriela Pratas, Francesco Ricci, Théo Richard, Chiara Sorrentino (apprentice)

FORMER COLLABORATORS

Eliana Barreto, Jessica Bertuzzi, Jonas Bornand, Marie-Laure Bourquin, Florian Bouvier, Marion Cruz, Alexandre Delencre, Guy Detruche, Ricardo Do Rego, Miguel Fernandes, Sven Hiestand, Téo Hubmann, Alfredo Huertas, Cindy Lachat, Cecilia Lante, Miruna Maldarescu, Lyes Mekroud, Kevin Navarro, Carlo Piffaretti, Andrea Riva, Santino Schepisi, Denis Sermaxhaj, Valeriya Todorova, Giacomo Giorgio Zwygart

CONFERENCES

2013	"Competition Vieusseux-Villars-Franchises – dialogues/exhibition", HEPIA, Geneva, May 15

BIBLIOGRAPHY

2008	Nicole Beetschen: "Séduisant projet pour réunir jeunes et vieux". In: *La Côte*, September 8, p.7 [Communal intergenerational building, Saint-Cergue]
2011	"Bois découverte". In: *Les visites Lignum*, p.12 [Mountain house, Leysin]
2013	"Vieusseux gagne 600 logements". In: *Tribune de Genève*, March 9 [Vieusseux-Villars-Franchises, Geneva]
	"Un nouvel espace de vie". In: *Bâtir*, April, p.8 [Vieusseux-Villars-Franchises, Geneva]
	"Le nouveau souffle d'une coopérative". In: *Le Temps*, April 3, p.19 [Vieusseux-Villars-Franchises, Geneva]
	Vincent Borcard: "Les ailes du désir". In: *Habitation*, No.2, June, p.4–9 [Vieusseux-Villars-Franchises, Geneva]
	Mary-Luce Boand Colombini: "De la chenillle au papillon". In: *Efficience 21*, No.7, June, p.8 [Vieusseux-Villars-Franchises, Geneva]
	"Des architectes genevois remportent un concours international". In: *Domotech*, No.3, June/July, p.6–11 [Vieusseux-Villars-Franchises, Geneva]
	"Aménagement des places publiques à Genève". In: *Interface*, No.18, July 4, p.26–27 [Vieusseux-Villars-Franchises, Geneva]
	Vincent Borcard: "Zusammenarbeit will gelernt sein". In: *Wohnen*, No.11, October 1, p.32–34 [Vieusseux-Villars-Franchises, Geneva]
	CHALETS. Trendsetting Mountain Treasures, Salenstein, p.202–205 [Mountain house, Leysin]
2016	"Le Servan fête ses 100 ans et construit pour l'avenir". In: *24 heures*, February 23 [Servan children's home, Lausanne]
2019	"Groupe scolaire des Vernets, Genève – Espaces multiusages". In: *hochparterre.wettbewerbe*, February, p.44–45 [Vernets School, Geneva]. *Cahiers suisses des concours d'architecture*, No.2, May
2019	Swiss Society of Engineers and Architects (SIA), Section Vaud (Ed.): *À voir, architectures romandes 2017–2019*, November, p.132 [Community hall and office spaces, Satigny]
2020	Christian Bernet: "La Ville aménage le futur espace entre Cornavin et le quartier des Grottes". In: *Geneva Tribune*, December 18, p.7 [Public spaces at Cornavin Main Station, Place de Montbrillant, Geneva]
	Gustavo Kuhn: "Le nord de la gare en plus vert et piéton". In: *Le Courrier*, December 18, p.5 [Public spaces at Cornavin Main Station, Place de Montbrillant, Geneva]

2021	Veronique Stein, «L'envers de la gare Cornavin s'offre un lifting» [Öffentlicher Raum am Bahnhof Cornavin, Place de Montbrillant, Genf], in: *Tout l'Immobilier*, 18. Januar, S. 12–13
	«Le futur gymnase du Chablais sera construit par des architectes genevois» [Kantonsschule Chablais, Aigle], unter: https://www.rts.ch/info/regions/vaud/12012525-le-futur-gymnase-du-chablais-sera-construit-par-des-architectes-genevois.html (zuletzt abgerufen: 9. Februar 2023)
	Isabelle Gay, «Aigle: le futur gymnase se dévoile» [Kantonsschule Chablais, Aigle], unter: https://www.lenouvelliste.ch/valais/chablais-valaisan/aigle-le-futur-gymnase-se-devoile-1051458 (zuletzt abgerufen: 9. Februar 2023)
	«Gymnase du Chablais: une ‹Rose des vents› a séduit le jury», unter: https://www.lacote.ch/vaud/la-cote/nyon-district/nyon-commune/gymnase-du-chablais-une-rose-des-vents-a-seduit-le-jury-1051471 (zuletzt abgerufen: 9. Februar 2023)
	David Genillard, «Le gymnase ‹Rose des vents› pourrait provoquer une tempête» [Kantonsschule Chablais, Aigle], in: *24 heures*, 2. März, S. 4
	«Le bois du futur gymnase du Chablais ne séduit guère son voisinage à Aigle» [Kantonsschule Chablais, Aigle], unter: https://www.batimag.ch/projets/le-bois-du-futur-gymnase-du-chablais-ne-seduit-guere-son-voisinage-a-aigle-3511 (zuletzt abgerufen: 9. Februar 2023)
	«Un gymnase en ‹Rose des vents›» [Kantonsschule Chablais, Aigle], unter: https://www.lacote.ch/vaud/la-cote/nyon-district/nyon-commune/gymnase-du-chablais-une-rose-des-vents-a-seduit-le-jury-1051471 (zuletzt aberufen: 9. Februar 2023)
	Camille Claessens-Vallet, «De quel bois le gymnase du futur est-il fait?» [Kantonsschule Chablais, Aigle], in: *Espazium*, 18. Mai, S. 54–58, siehe auch: https://www.espazium.ch/fr/actualites/de-quel-bois-le-gymnase-du-futur-est-il-fait#:~:text=Le%20gymnase%20du%20futur%20°st%20low%2Dtech%20°t%20tectonique&text=Le%20reste%20de%20la%20ˢᵗructure%20sera%20°n%20bois%20massif (zuletzt abgerufen: 9. Februar 2023)
2022	«Une maison comme les autres» [Kinderheim Servan, Lausanne], in: *Construction & Bâtiment*, Nr. 2, S. 34–37
	[Kinderheim Servan, Lausanne], in: Schweizerischer Ingenieur- und Architektenverein (SIA), Sektion Waadt (Hrsg.), *À voir, architectures romandes 2019–2022*, S. 26–27
	Sylvain Muller, «Le gymnase du futur sera organique, multi-usages et écolo», in: *24 heures*, 22. Dezember, S. 5, [Kantonsschule Chablais, Aigle]

DIDIER CHALLAND
Textbeitrag

1969	Geboren in Fribourg
1989–1996	Diplom an der École Polytechnique Fédérale de Lausanne (EPFL) bei Professor Martin Steinmann
1992–1994	Praktikum bei Benedict Tonon, Berlin
1994	Praktikum bei O.M. Ungers, Berlin
1996–1998	Architekt bei Philippe Gueissaz, Sainte-Croix, Waadt
1999–2000	Architekt bei M+B Zurbuchen-Henz, Lausanne
2000–2001	Assistent des Gastprofessors Philippe Gueissaz, EPFL
2000–	Beginn der freiberuflichen Tätigkeit
2001–2008	Assistent von Professor Martin Steinmann, EPFL
2010	Doktor der Wissenschaften an der EPFL
2010–	Dozent für Planung und Theorie, HEPIA Genf

DANK

Nach 25 Jahren der Zusammenarbeit und 15-jährigem Bestehen des Büros hat uns diese Publikation einen wertvollen Rückblick auf unsere berufliche Karriere ermöglicht. Wir danken Linus Wirz ganz herzlich für sein Vertrauen und seinen Enthusiasmus sowie allen Mitarbeitenden des Quart Verlags.

Dank gilt auch Didier Challand, einem Freund und Kollegen seit vielen Jahren, für seinen einfühlsamen Blick auf unsere architektonische Arbeit, sein offenes Ohr, seine Fragen und seine kostbare Zeit, die er diesem Werk gewidmet hat.

Wir möchten an dieser Stelle unseren früheren und heutigen Kolleginnen und Kollegen unseren Dank und unsere Anerkennung für ihr tägliches grosses Engagement aussprechen, ohne das unsere Arbeit ganz einfach nicht existieren würde. Wir danken unserer Praktikantin Caroline David und unserem Praktikanten Téo Hubmann, die an der Vorbereitung der hier veröffentlichten Pläne umfassend beteiligt waren, und wir wünschen ihnen viel Erfolg für ihren weiteren beruflichen Werdegang.

Dieses Buch hätte ohne die aufmerksame Lektüre der Texte im Kollegen- und Freundeskreis nicht das Licht der Welt erblickt. Wir danken in diesem Zusammenhang insbesondere Adela García-Herrera, die sich neben ihrer Übersetzung ins Spanische auch sonst intensiv für das Werk eingesetzt hat; aber auch Brigitte Werder-Jermann und Maria Naenny, die uns für die deutsche Fassung mit gutem Rat zur Seite standen.

Bei unserer Arbeit nehmen das Gehör und die Zusammenarbeit mit den Bauherrschaften, Institutionen, Auftragnehmenden, Firmen und Handwerkerinnen und Handwerkern einen wesentlichen Platz ein: Teamarbeit ist für die Realisierung der Projekte unverzichtbar. Wir danken ihnen allen bei dieser Gelegenheit für die unentwegte Unterstützung, ihre Kenntnisse und ihre Hilfe. Ein grosses Dankeschön gilt insbesondere auch denen, die durch ihre grosszügige finanzielle Förderung zum Erscheinen dieser Publikation beigetragen haben. Unser architektonisches Wirken und unser Privatleben sind eng miteinander verknüpft. Wir wollen hier nicht unsere Angehörigen und Familien vergessen, die uns mit ihrer Hilfe, mitunter auch einfach mit ihrer puren Präsenz, aber vor allem mit ihrer Ermutigung und ihrer Kritik begleiten und uns erlauben, voranzuschreiten. Jedes Projekt ist ein menschliches Abenteuer, das uns Tag für Tag erfreut und motiviert. Danke.

2021	Veronique Stein: "L'envers de la gare Cornavin s'offre un lifting". In: *Tout l'Immobilier*, January 18, p. 12–13 [Public spaces at Cornavin Main Station, Place de Montbrillant, Geneva]
	"Le futur gymnase du Chablais sera construit par des architectes genevois". In: *RTS Info,* March 1 [Chablais High School, Aigle], https://www.rts.ch/info/regions/vaud/12012525-le-futur-gymnase-du-chablais-sera-construit-par-des-architectes-genevois.html (last accessed: February 9, 2023)
	Isabelle Gay: "Aigle: le futur gymnase se dévoile". In: *Le Nouvelliste,* March 1: https://www.lenouvelliste.ch/valais/chablais-valaisan/aigle-le-futur-gymnase-se-devoile-1051458 (last accessed: February 9, 2023) [Chablais High School, Aigle]
	"Gymnase du Chablais: une 'Rose des vents' a séduit le jury". In: *La Côte,* March 1, p. 4: https://www.lacote.ch/vaud/la-cote/nyon-district/nyon-commune/gymnase-du-chablais-une-rose-des-vents-a-seduit-le-jury-1051471 [Chablais High School, Aigle] (last accessed: February 9, 2023)
	David Genillard: "Le gymnase 'Rose des vents' pourrait provoquer une tempête". In: *24 heures,* March 2: https://www.24heures.ch/le-gymnase-rose-des-vents-pourrait-provoquer-une-tempete-260091728729 [Chablais High School, Aigle] (last accessed: February 9, 2023)
	"Le bois du futur gymnase du Chablais ne séduit guère son voisinage à Aigle". In: *Batimag,* March 2: https://www.batimag.ch/projets/le-bois-du-futur-gymnase-du-chablais-ne-seduit-guere-son-voisinage-a-aigle-3511 [Chablais High School, Aigle] (last accessed: February 9, 2023)
	"Un gymnase en 'Rose des vents'". In: *La Côte,* March 6 [Chablais High School, Aigle], https://www.espazium.ch/fr/actualites/de-quel-bois-le-gymnase-du-futur-est-il-fait#:~:text=Le%20gymnase%20du%20futur%20est%20low%2Dtech%20et%20tectonique&text=Le%20reste%20de%20la%20structure%20sera%20en%20bois%20massif (last accessed: February 9, 2023)
	Camille Claessens-Vallet: "De quel bois le gymnase du futur est-il fait?". In: *Espazium,* May 18, p. 54–58 [Chablais High School, Aigle], https://www.espazium.ch/fr/actualites/de-quel-bois-le-gymnase-du-futur-est-il-fait#:~:text=Le%20gymnase%20du%20futur%20ᵉst%20low%2Dtech%20ᵗt%20tectonique&text=Le%20reste%20de%20la%20ˢᵗructure%20sera%20ᵉⁿ%20bois%20massif (last accessed: February 9, 2023)
2022	Espaces Contemporains (Ed.): "Une maison comme les autres". In: *Construction & Bâtiment,* No. 2, April/May, p. 34–37 [Servan children's home, Lausanne]
	SIA Section Vaud (Ed.): *À voir, architectures romandes 2019–2022*, November, p. 26–27 [Servan children's home, Lausanne]
	Sylvain Muller: "Le gymnase du futur sera organique, multi-usages et écolo", dans: *24 heures,* December 22, p. 5, [Chablais High School, Aigle]

DIDIER CHALLAND
Article

1969	Born in Fribourg
1989–1996	École Polytechnique Fédérale de Lausanne (EPFL) diploma under Professor Martin Steinmann
1992–1994	Internship at Benedict Tonon, Berlin
1994	Internship at O.M. Ungers, Berlin
1996–1998	Architect at Philippe Gueissaz, Sainte-Croix VD
1999–2000	Architect at M+B Zurbuchen-Henz, Lausanne
2000–2001	Assistant to Visiting Professor Philippe Gueissaz, EPFL
2000–	Start of self-employment
2001–2008	Assistant to Professor Martin Steinmann, EPFL
2010	Doctor of Science, EPFL
2010–	Senior Lecturer, Project and Theory, HEPIA Geneva

ACKNOWLEDGEMENTS

After 25 years of close and distant partnership and 15 years of independent office work, we have been able to reflect on our professional careers with this publication. We extend our sincere gratitude to the entire Quart publishing staff as well as Linus Wirz for his confidence and zeal.

We are grateful to Didier Challand, a long-time friend and confidant in the field, for his thoughtful assessment of our architectural approach, his listening, his questioning and his priceless time devoted to this work.

Our work simply would not exist without the tremendous everyday dedication of our colleagues, both past and present, so we would like to extend our gratitude and admiration to them. Special thanks to Caroline David and Téo Hubmann, two of our interns who contributed significantly to the creation of the published drawings, and we wish them the best of luck in their future academic endeavours.

This work would not have been published without its meticulous, friendly and professional text editing. Adela Garca-Herrera deserves special recognition because she contributed significantly beyond just translating into Spanish, as well as Brigitte Werder-Jermann and Maria Naenny, who provided good advice on the German version.

Our technique involves a strong emphasis on working closely with customers, institutions, contractors, businesses and employees, since successful project completion requires teamwork. We would like to take this opportunity to express our gratitude for their ongoing assistance, knowledge and cooperation. Additional gratitude is due to those who kindly sponsored and financed the publication of this work.

Our personal lives and the practice of architecture are closely related. We do not forget our families and close friends who support us and help us advance by their assistance, sometimes just by being there, but mostly through their encouragement and criticism.

Every project we work on is a human adventure that inspires and enthuses us every day. Many thanks for your support. Thanks.

FINANZIELLE UND IDEELLE UNTERSTÜTZUNG

Ein besonderer Dank gilt den Institutionen und Sponsorfirmen, deren finanzielle Unterstützungen wesentlich zum Entstehen dieser Buchreihe beitragen. Ihr kulturelles Engagement ermöglicht ein fruchtbares und freundschaftliches Zusammenwirken von Baukultur und Bauwirtschaft.

FINANCIAL AND CONCEPTUAL SUPPORT

Special thanks to our sponsors and institutions whose financial support has helped us so much with the production of this series of books. Their cultural commitment is a valuable contribution to fruitful and cordial collaboration between the culture and economics of architecture.

Schweizerische Eidgenossenschaft
Confédération suisse
Confederazione Svizzera
Confederaziun svizra

Eidgenössisches Departement des Innern EDI
Bundesamt für Kultur BAK

EDMS Ingénieurs SA, Petit Lancy

Empty

EMPTY SL, Madrid

Prelco SA, Satigny

Société Coopérative d'Habitation Genève

UNeO

UNEO SA, Carouge

AAV Contractors SA, Plan-les-Ouates
AB Ingénieurs SA, Thônex
Abvent SA, Estavayer-le-Lac
AcouConsult Sàrl, Genève
Atelier Guggisberg, Lausanne
Cerutti Toitures SA, Les Acacias

Conti & Associés Ingénieurs SA, Versoix
D'Orlando GPI SA, Vésenaz
Dasta Charpentes-Bois SA, Plan-les-Ouates
Di Chiara SA, Vernier
FLPAI, Fondation des Logements pour Personnes Âgées ou Isolées, Genève

Jobin SA, Lausanne
Licht+Raum AG, Ittigen
Mémoire Vive SA, Lausanne/Fribourg
Rampini & Cie SA, Vernier
Swisspro SR SA, Le Lignon
Weinmann Energies SA, Echallens

Giorgis Rodriguez
101. Band der Reihe *De aedibus*
Herausgegeben von: Heinz Wirz, Luzern
Konzept: Heinz Wirz; Giorgis Rodriguez, Genf
Projektleitung: Quart Verlag, Linus Wirz
Textbeitrag: Didier Challand, Lausanne
Objekttexte: Giorgis Rodriguez
Textlektorat deutsch: Miriam Seifert-Waibel, Hamburg
Textlektorat englisch: Benjamin Liebelt, Berlin
Übersetzung französisch–deutsch: Dr. Eva Dewes, Saarbrücken
Übersetzung französisch–englisch: Beate Ummenhofer, language service, Wien
Fotos: Julien Barro, Genf, S. 17, 19; Yves André, Vaumarcus, S. 21–25; Laura Keller, Genf, S. 27–31; Olivier Di Giambattista, Genf, S. 33–35; Roger Frei, Zürich, S. 40–43, 45–49; Giorgis Rodriguez Architectes, S. 18, 36, 38, 39, 53, 58–63, 76 (Nr. 1,2,4,5), 81
Visualisierungen: Camera Picta, Genf/Treviso, S. 37, 77 (Nr. 9); Filippo Bolognese Images, Milan/Mendrisio, S. 55–57; MAP-Paysage, Lausanne, S. 54, 56–57; Imagine We Create, Matosinhos, S. 51–52, 65, 67, 69–71, 73–75, 76 (Nr. 3), 77 (Nr. 6, 8); Playtime, Barcelona, S. 77 (Nr. 7); Nightnurse Images, Zürich, S. 77 (Nr. 10)
Redesign: BKVK, Basel – Beat Keusch, Angelina Köpplin-Stützle
Grafische Umsetzung: Quart Verlag Luzern
Lithos: Printeria, Luzern
Druck: DZA Druckerei zu Altenburg GmbH

Der Quart Verlag wird vom Bundesamt für Kultur für die Jahre 2021–2024 unterstützt.

© Copyright 2023
Quart Verlag Luzern, Heinz Wirz
Alle Rechte vorbehalten
ISBN 978-3-03761-256-9

Dieses Buch ist auch auf spanisch/französisch erschienen: ISBN 978-3-03761-280-4

Giorgis Rodriguez
Volume 101 of the series *De aedibus*
Edited by: Heinz Wirz, Lucerne
Concept: Heinz Wirz; Giorgis Rodriguez, Geneva
Project management: Quart Verlag, Linus Wirz
Article by: Didier Challand, Lausanne
Project descriptions: Giorgis Rodriguez
German text editing: Miriam Seifert-Waibel, Hamburg
English text editing: Benjamin Liebelt, Berlin
French – German translation: Dr. Eva Dewes, Saarbrücken
French – English translation: Beate Ummenhofer, language service, Vienna
Photos: Julien Barro, Geneva, p. 17, 19; Yves André, Vaumarcus, p. 21–25; Laura Keller, Geneva, p. 27–31; Olivier Di Giambattista, Geneva, p. 33–35; Roger Frei, Zurich, p. 40–43, 45–49; Giorgis Rodriguez Architectes, p. 18, 36, 38, 39, 53, 58–63, 76 (Nos. 1,2,4,5), 81
Visualisations: Camera Picta, Geneva/Treviso, p. 37, 77 (No. 9); Filippo Bolognese Images, Milan/Mendrisio, p. 55–57; MAP-Paysage, Lausanne, p. 54, 56–57; Imagine We Create, Matosinhos, p. 51–52, 65, 67, 69–71, 73–75, 76 (No. 3), 77 (Nos. 6,8); Playtime, Barcelona, p. 77 (No. 7); Nightnurse Images, Zurich, p. 77 (No. 10)
Redesign: BKVK, Basel – Beat Keusch, Angelina Köpplin-Stützle
Graphic design: Quart Verlag Luzern
Lithos: Printeria, Lucerne
Printing: DZA Druckerei zu Altenburg GmbH

Quart Publishers is being supported by the Federal Office of Culture for the years 2021–2024.

© Copyright 2023
Quart Verlag Luzern, Heinz Wirz
All rights reserved
ISBN 978-3-03761-256-9

Also published in Spanish/French:
ISBN 978-3-03761-280-4

Quart Verlag GmbH
Denkmalstrasse 2, CH-6006 Luzern
books@quart.ch, www.quart.ch

De aedibus
Zeitgenössische Architekturschaffende und ihre Bauten

De aedibus
Contemporary architects and their buildings

101	Giorgis Rodriguez (de/en, es/fr)	50	Luca Gazzaniga (de/en)
100	Carlos Martinez (de/en)	49	Guignard & Saner (de/en)
99	Stocker Lee (de/en, it)	48	Morger + Dettli (de/en)
98	Roman Hutter (de/en)	47	Charles Pictet (de/en)
97	Bachelard Wagner (de/en, fr)	46	Armando Ruinelli + Partner (de/en/it)
96	Alain Wolff architectes (de/en, fr)	45	Luca Selva Architekten (de/en)
95	Horisberger Wagen (de/en)	44	Luca Deon (de/en)
94	Pont12 (de/en, fr)	43	2b (de/en)
93	Christian Dupraz (de/en, fr)	42	Durisch + Nolli (de/en)
92	group8 (de/en, fr/en)	41	sabarchitekten (de/en)
91	MPH (de/en, fr/en)	40	Beat Rothen (de/en)
90	Spillmann Echsle (de/en)	39	Atelier Bonnet (de/en)
89	Andy Senn (de/en)	38	Novaron (de/en)
88	Architetti Tibiletti Associati (de/en)	37	Althammer Hochuli (de/en)
87	Zach + Zünd (de/en)	36	Schneider & Schneider (de/en)
86	Kistler Vogt (de/en)	35	Frei & Ehrensperger (de, en)
85	Sylla Widmann (de/en, fr/en)	34	Liechti Graf Zumsteg (de/en)
84	Aebi & Vincent Architekten (de/en)	33	Adrian Streich (de/en)
83	Baumberger & Stegmeier (de/en)	32	Daniele Marques (de/en)
82	L-architectes (de/en, de/fr)	31	Neff Neumann (de/en)
81	Frei Rezakhanlou (de/en)	30	Giraudi Wettstein (de/en)
80	weberbrunner (de/en)	29	Steinmann & Schmid (de/en)
79	Meyer Piattini (de/en)	28	Matthias Ackermann (de/en)
78	meier + associés architectes (de/en, de/fr)	27	Aeby & Perneger (de/en)
77	Lin Robbe Seiler (de/en, de/fr)	26	Bakker & Blanc (de/en)
76	Meier Leder (de/en)	25	Markus Wespi Jérôme de Meuron (de/en)
75	Butikofer de Oliveira Vernay (de/en)	24	Bauart (de/en, de/fr)
74	Elisabeth & Martin Boesch (de/en)	23	Knapkiewicz & Fickert (de/en)
73	spaceshop Architekten (de/en)	22	Marcel Ferrier (de/en)
72	Kast Kaeppeli (de/en)	21	Wild Bär Architekten (de/en)
71	Philippe Meyer (de/en, fr)	20	Enzmann + Fischer (de/en)
70	bartbuchhofer (de/en)	19	Mierta und Kurt Lazzarini (de/en)
69	Hauenstein La Roche Schedler (de/en)	18	Rolf Mühlethaler (de/en)
68	Graeme Mann & Patricia Capua Mann (de/en)	17	Pablo Horváth (de/en)
67	Esposito Javet (de/en, de/fr)	16	Brauen + Wälchli (de/en)
66	Galletti Matter (de/en, de/fr)	15	E2A Eckert Eckert Architekten (de/en)
65	Fruehauf, Henry & Viladoms (de/en)	14	Lussi + Halter (de/en)
64	Jakob Steib (de/en)	13	Philipp Brühwiler (de/en)
63	bunq (de/en)	12	Scheitlin – Syfrig + Partner (de/en)
62	Jean-Paul Jaccaud (de/en, de/fr)	11	Vittorio Magnago Lampugnani (de/en)
61	huggenbergerfries (de/en)	10	Bonnard Woeffray (de/en, de/fr)
60	Berrel Berrel Kräutler (de/en)	9	Graber Pulver (de/en)
59	Pierre-Alain Dupraz (de/en, de/fr)	8	Burkhalter Sumi / Makiol Wiederkehr (de/en)
58	Cometti Truffer (de/en)	7	Gigon/Guyer (de, en)
57	Joos & Mathys (de/en)	6	Andrea Bassi (de, fr, en)
56	Lacroix Chessex (de/en)	5	Dieter Jüngling und Andreas Hagmann (de, en)
55	Savioz Fabrizzi (de/en, de/fr)	4	Beat Consoni (de/en)
54	Boegli Kramp (de/en)	3	Max Bosshard & Christoph Luchsinger (de)
53	Zita Cotti (de/en)	2	Miroslav Šik (de, en, it)
52	Oestreich + Schmid (de/en)	1	Valentin Bearth & Andrea Deplazes (de, en, it)
51	Stump & Schibli Architekten (de/en)		

books@quart.ch, www.quart.ch